THE MAKING OF
Disney's
ANIMAL
KINGDOM™
THEME PARK

THE MAKING OF
DISNEY'S
ANIMAL
KINGDOM™
THEME PARK

MELODY
MALMBERG

This book is dedicated to my husband, my sons, and my mother, with thanks and love.

A Roundtable Press Book

New York

ACKNOWLEDGMENTS
Let me start with a generalization:
*Everyone involved with Disney's Animal Kingdom™ Theme Park has shown an incredible dedication not just to their own jobs
but to the project as a whole. They are articulate and passionate about their work. I benefited from people's generosity.
They freely shared their thoughts and time, notes, drawings, and photos in the midst of the controlled craziness
that is designing, building, and running a theme park.
As always at Disney, the support staff extended their help to me, an outsider, without stinting.
My thanks to Wendy Lefkon, who took a chance on me and my first "real" book,
to Gene Duncan for providing many wonderful images, and to Steven Rosen for putting them all together.
This book had its genesis in the fertile brain of Pamela Fisher, my friend, encourager, and sometimes colleague for nearly a decade and a half.
Of course, I could not have written this without my husband, Joe Rohde: without him, there wouldn't be anything to write about.
Joe's love for and belief in me, coupled with his willingness to help with everything from editing to baby-sitting,
made the whole thing thinkable, doable, and even publishable.
Finally, thanks to Kellan for helping me identify dinosaurs, and to both Kellan and (no longer baby) Brandt for making me smile.*

Photographs used in Chapter 8 are courtesy of:
*Cynthia Moss and Rebecca Villarreal, African Wildlife Foundation; Kiki Arnal and Russell Thorstrom, The Peregrine Fund;
Eduardo Nycander, Charles Munn, and John Hart, Wildlife Conservation Fund; Thomas Butynski, Zoo Atlanta;
Jeff Lumm, Zoological Society of San Diego; John Lukas, International Rhino Foundation.*

For Hyperion
Editor: Wendy Lefkon
Assistant Editor: Robin Friedman

For Roundtable Press, Inc.
Directors: Susan E. Meyer, Marsha Melnick
Design Concept: Michaelis/Carpelis Design
Text: Melody Malmberg
Editor: Patricia Fogarty
Manufacturing Consultant: Bill Rose
Project Coordinator, Computer Production, Photo Editor, Designer: Steven Rosen

ISBN 0-7868-6402-8
First Edition
2 4 6 8 10 9 7 5 3 1

CONTENTS

INTRODUCTION

As this introduction is being written, there are thousands of people walking around inside Disney's Animal Kingdom™ Theme Park. They are riding our attractions, eating in our restaurants, enjoying the ambience of the most lush landscape we have ever created. They see a place that is to all appearances complete. Barely a hint remains to suggest that the forests and savannahs of Africa have not been there for centuries, that the moldering buildings of DinoLand, U.S.A., have not seen decades of use, that the Tree of Life rising over the center of the park has not been growing forever.

The completeness is hypnotic. It disguises the truth about everything those first invited guests see: that all this—every wall, every color, every object, even the plants, the animals, the earth beneath their feet—all this was created or collected and brought together through the agency of vast human effort. That effort has taken nearly a decade of some of our lives and involved hundreds of Imagineers and thousands of construction workers. It has sent people across the planet acquiring the knowledge, the experience, the talent, and the materials out of which this amazing creation was made.

That story is invisible to those who see Disney's Animal Kingdom Theme Park only as a finished product, a world complete in itself. We who were the creators of this place will always see it in another way, as a result of our ideas, our labor, our trials and errors, our victories, of our combined talents, our dedication, and of the years of our lives invested in seeing this project through.

Perhaps, after reading this book, you too will be able to perceive us as you look at the cast of sunlight on a faded plaster wall, or hear a dinosaur roar in the moonlight of prehistoric night, or watch an antelope leap across a grassy plain, or contemplate the flutter of a blossom on a wind-tossed tree. Perhaps you will be able to sense us still there, incorporated forever into the magic of our created kingdom. And you may ask why? Why such effort, so many years, such dedication to a mere idea?

It is for you. You who come to this place to experience the adventure, the excitement, the challenge, and the joy of the world of animals. And it is for them, the animals themselves. It is my hope, and I believe all of ours, that we have created a place that will awaken our hearts to the beauty and wonder of the creatures that surround us, and renew our dedication to conserving those places on Earth where they may survive until a wiser time when we have learned the lessons of the Earth and can share in harmony with our partners on this small planet, the animals.

Joe Rohde
Executive Designer,
Disney's Animal Kingdom Theme Park

CLEAR BLUE SKY

❝You know,
we have the
Magic Kingdom.
We should have
Disney's Animal
Kingdom.❞

MICHAEL EISNER,
WALT DISNEY COMPANY CEO

*Opposite: any blank piece of paper,
even Disney letterhead, is fair game
for Imagineers sketching ideas for a
theme park. The layout of crucial
elements helps heighten guest expectations. This sequence shows how
low-lying elements protect a view of
a major attraction in a proposed
fantasy section of Disney's Animal
Kingdom™ Theme Park. Background:
notes on animal requirements com-
pete with cartoon images.*

It wasn't particularly high on the Walt Disney Company's 1989 "to do" list: a theme park about animals. Chairman Michael Eisner had tried out various concepts in surveys of theme park guests, and "Disney and animals" always tested strongly. But an analysis of the economics of zoo attractions was disappointing: zoos didn't make money.

Yet the synergy between Disney and animals was undeniable. Disney made animals lovable in countless films and cartoons. The Oscar-winning *True-Life Adventures* series (1948–1960) practically invented the nature documentary. And one of Walt's most-quoted aphorisms was "I only hope that we never lose sight of one thing—that it was all started by a mouse."

Eisner decided that, despite the economics, the project should go to Walt Disney Imagineering—Disney's design staff, the wizards who built Disneyland® Park in California and its descendants in Orlando, Tokyo, and Paris. The Imagineering designers, writers, architects, engineers, and technicians—consummate storytellers in three dimensions—think up and build the Disney attractions and adventures, including the parks' *Audio-Animatronics*® characters, ride systems, and 3-D movies.

In January 1990, Imagineering concept designer Joe Rohde, whose work included the Adventurers Club at Downtown Disney Pleasure Island, had an initial meeting with Eisner about the animal park. As Rohde drove his pickup from the Glendale, California, offices of Imagineering to the corporate headquarters in Burbank, he had an inspiration: the park would have three equal components—traditional theme park, Epcot®-style pavilion, and nontraditional zoo.

He pitched the idea to Eisner, who agreed on that basic framework and urged Rohde to include emotion, theatrics, and storytelling to reach people. Eisner also mused about the name: "You know, we have the Magic Kingdom. We should have Disney's Animal Kingdom."

"We called it that from then on," remembers Rohde. The "blue sky effort"—Imagineering's initial open-ended exploration of a concept—began. With a name, a three-part idea, and 12 weeks to come up with the broad outlines of a new theme park, Rohde assembled a tiny team for the long-shot project. "They had just announced the Disney Decade—

including a list of new parks and attractions scheduled to debut before the year 2000—and we were *not* in it," Rohde recalls.

The six-member team set up shop on February 1 in a minuscule conference room in a temporary office trailer parked on the Imagineering lot. It had a table and a display board and piles of books and blank index cards. The team took the words "animal" and "kingdom" and brainstormed for two or three weeks. The Imagineers spent their free time reading books and watching animal documentaries. They culled out a broad, rich list of ideas that fit the three categories. "Were we to go back to those original

ideas," Rohde confides, "we would definitely find stuff we could use today."

The objective was to give Eisner an idea and theme for the park, and to show him how the idea broke down into locations that could be built. The idea that kept welling up was that animals were the catalyst for fascination, projection, and involvement. It was an overwhelmingly positive idea, something around which they could build stories—and a whole theme park. The park was not to be only about animals, but also about people's emotional reaction to animals. It was not to be an information park or an issues park, but a park about love.

ANIMALS AS ACTORS

Walt Disney had initially considered live animal actors for Disneyland. But to get a consistent presentation so that every guest saw the same well-choreographed show, he had to rely on robots. The continual nature of shows like the Jungle Cruise and Nature's Wonderland—with key scenes like elks butting heads and elephants spraying the boats— were impossible to stage consistently without inventing new animation technology.

Forty years later, the theme park world had changed along with American culture. People wanted a less rigid, more

individualized experience at a theme park, and live animals were a definite draw. But Disney wouldn't do a park just about live animals. The concept was broadened, to bring the talents of the storytellers at Imagineering to the world of animals.

THE CORE TEAM: DECIDEDLY DIFFERENT

Disney's Animal Kingdom™ Theme Park emphatically was not going to be a traditional theme park, so Imagineering team leader Joe Rohde assembled a group with diversified design experience. They had worked together on Downtown Disney Pleasure Island and had just come off a postponed Imagineering development project for urban entertainment centers. Rohde's Occidental College roommate, writer Kevin Brown, had honed his skills at the California Renaissance Faires as a director and performer. Zofia Kostyrko, a concept designer, had a background in fine arts, film, and television. Tony Marando was a set designer whose experience was mostly on Broadway. Interior designer Christopher West was assigned as project architect. Patsy Tillisch, a former Six Flags theme park operations manager who had been an executive secretary in Disney's corporate offices, was assigned to be the administrative assistant for the team.

The initial members of the Imagineering team (standing, left to right) Zofia Kostyrko, Kevin Brown, Christopher West, Tony Marando, and (seated) Joe Rohde; not shown is Patsy Tillisch.

66 *From the very beginning, there was a strong sense that time was running out for animals. And there was always an awareness that if Disney did this, they had to do it right.* 99

ZOFIA KOSTYRKO,
SENIOR CONCEPT DESIGNER

LOVE IS IT

For the Imagineers, love for animals fell into three stages corresponding to human development. As kids, our love of animals comes from fantasy, myth, and stories. "A child's love of animals is self-centered, anthropomorphic, projected," explains chief designer Joe Rohde, sounding like the psychology teacher he briefly was. "It's the world of stuffed animals, first pets, fairy tales.

"In adolescence, a love of animals is expressed by adventure, a longing to have a physical experience of them. Kids are excited by animals; they want to know about them, be like them, be with them. As adults, our love of animals grows more intellectual. This mature, respectful love is expressed as appreciation, understanding, protection."

The team related the three stages of love for animals to the new project. The child's love of animals became theme-park and fantasy elements. The adolescent desire for experience became the safari adventure/zoo side. Adults' love for animals inspired Epcot pavilion-like ideas.

Being an animal was an important early concept. Thus was born the idea of presenting animals as naturally as possible, with no visible barriers between them and guests. Adventure was another big piece of the puzzle. Guests would again and again be challenged by doable adventures. It would not be only the attractions; the gritty look of the proposed villages suggested that something real could happen. Even the park entry was planned as an adventure—not a traditional broad thoroughfare that orients you to the park, but an opaque, transforming environment that must be explored in order to be appreciated.

The animals would be there to be admired, but guests would constantly be reminded of the frailty of human endeavor in the face of nature. The designers deliberately suppressed the scale of the architecture, using folk styles instead of national monuments, making it aged, smothering it in foliage. Nature's transcendent power would be felt throughout the entire park.

66 *We assumed that nobody is indifferent to animals. Everyone has strong feelings about them, usually positive ones. We chose love. We never found it strange, unusual, or weird, because it was true. We weren't uncomfortable with love as a concept—it was boldly stated. Nobody perceived it as mushy. And love as an idea became a skeleton for everything else.* **99**

ZOFIA KOSTYRKO,
SENIOR CONCEPT DESIGNER

As the Imagineers played with broad concepts, they also came up with a variety of basic notions for the park's shape. Like Disneyland and the Magic Kingdom, Disney's Animal Kingdom Theme Park would have, in "bubble diagram" format, a radial, hub-and-spoke plan. There would be an icon at the hub or center of the park, with broad "spokes" of safaris and experiences running out from it. In the early days, each of the three areas—fantasy, zoo, and pavilion—carried equal weight.

The first presentation of the Animal Kingdom project to Walt Disney Company CEO Michael Eisner and president Frank Wells was a simple board covered with 3x5 cards. Overall, the executives were intrigued by the key concept, the love of animals, and the notion that, in the Animal Kingdom park, nature would be more powerful than human effort.
Left: an early concept for a topiary castle, part of the fantasy area.
Below: the original icon—a three-tier carousel—was vetoed by Eisner. "He thought it was too frivolous," remembers Joe Rohde. "Already he had a sense of the mission of the place."

As they finished work on the fantasy areas, the team turned to the design of the Epcot-style pavilion. They toured successful exhibits at zoos, museums, and aquariums, and adapted ideas from the interactive Wonders of Life attractions.
Above: what began as a single large pavilion became a land interspersed with smaller buildings filled with shows, rides, and interactive devices. The driving philosophy was entertainment.
Right: early ideas for interactive attractions included opportunities to BE an animal—to see like a chameleon, bug, or eagle, or to hear like a bat.

START WITH WHAT YOU KNOW

Having passed the initial hurdle, the Imagineers laid out a development strategy for the park: they would start with what they knew and move toward what they did not know. They began designing fantasy theme park elements while researching animal care, zoos, and safaris, and making initial contacts in the zoo world.

Kym Murphy is a biologist and Disney's corporate vice president for environmental policy. When the Imagineers asked for advice, Kym suggested Dr. Bill Conway of the New York Zoological Society. Conway "was a visionary," says Joe Rohde. "He had way more ambitious ideas than we did about animals and habitats—how you

could mix different species of animals in the same habitat, how close guests could come to animals." Conway introduced the team to the American Zoo and Aquarium Association and their Species Survival Plans, which help birthrates improve dramatically by arranging exchanges of animals among zoos. Conway began the Imagineers' long education on animal acquisition, exhibition, husbandry, and research.

Understanding that layout and landscape were becoming critical to the project, Rohde asked a landscape planner, John Shields, and a landscape architect, Paul Comstock, to join the team. Together, they journeyed to Walt Disney World® Resort to check out available sites.

The Imagineering team fell in love with the possibilities of the land at the far west of Walt Disney World. It was high, dry, and almost entirely second-use; in mid-1990 it was a cow pasture and settling ponds, the site of the Disney tree farm and fireworks testing ground. Stands of native oaks on the land could be saved and worked into outdoor safaris, and native populations of birds and animals could be relocated.

An operations liaison, Eric Eberhart, helped the team size rides and pathways and plan the layout of attractions, and got them thinking about where cast members would dress and how guests would move around the park. The Imagineers visited zoos and animal facilities, paying attention to naturalistic exhibits and areas of contact between guests and animals, noting what worked and what didn't. They talked to keepers and gift shop clerks. And each time they returned to Imagineering, they had to explain how and why Disney's Animal Kingdom Theme Park would *not* be a zoo.

Above: John Shields consults the proposed safari layout from the vantage point of a helicopter. Right: the first Imagineers to visit the site document it with film, video, and sketches; clockwise from top: Ben Tripp, Joe Rohde, Zofia Kostyrko, and Paul Comstock.

THE GRAND MASTER PLAN

Creating a master plan for Disney's Animal Kingdom Theme Park began almost as soon as the designers convened for the first time. In the earliest design phase, all ideas were out on the table. A mature park 20 years from opening date was laid out in its ideal form.

Wetlands—Boggy Creek on the west and Reedy Creek on the east—hemmed in the long and narrow park site on both sides. Planned and existing roads, visual intrusion from off-site high-rises, and natural features like existing trees helped dictate the layout of the park.

Starting at the center, with the Tree of Life, project landscape planner John Shields determined how much land was needed for Safari Village, then drew the inner edge of Discovery River. The width of the river determined the placement of the "lands" and the service road, a ring road that circles the park and lets employees move around "backstage." Far from defining the perimeter of the park, the service road is considered movable; it can be located even farther out if more land is required within its bounds.

When designing the appearance of Camp Minnie–Mickey, a land conceived while the park was being built, Imagineers consulted the master plan. Since the camp was located just to the north of the unbuilt animal fantasy area, the theme for Camp Minnie–Mickey had to serve as a bridge from Safari Village to the planned home of mythical beasts and legendary creatures. The solution, an Adirondack-themed area, will harmonize with both neighboring lands.

The team planned well, utilizing the wetlands to the west and the Disney tree farm in the north to expand the views of the African savannah off-site. But master plans are not foolproof. A deep corridor of utilities was installed underground, skirting Discovery River. In the master plan, the Asian safari was located well out from the utilities, but it was shifted closer to the river as the concept changed from expansive river safari to white-water thrills. It was impossible to build the massive Asia mountain over the utilities, so the lines had to be dug up, structurally supported, and reburied before construction could begin.

INTO AFRICA

As designs for the "known" areas of the park progressed, the team of Imagineers confronted the fact that an African safari was high on the list of probable attractions for opening day.

The Imagineers knew that the safari component needed to be authentic. They reasoned that their major "competition" would be Africa itself. They researched family-oriented package trips, from the lowest to the highest end, then created their own East African itinerary. It was to be an exposure to what a family might be able to do as a once-in-a-lifetime experience.

In July 1990, the team took off for Africa on a rough, disorganized, incredible trip to Kenya and Tanzania. The two-week trek was characterized by breathtaking animal encounters, and smaller planes. The group was overloaded with video and still cameras. In one tiny plane, designers were buried in luggage up to their necks.

The research trip to Africa served both as a documentary and a wellspring for creativity. For instance, no photograph, no video can capture the elusive color of the kopjes (pronounced "koppies"), the big, rounded rocks that are so characteristic of the African plains. Formed of granite, they have a subtle undertone of pink that disappears on film but makes them unique. The Imagineers took many rolls of slides that framed African scenes of the look and size they could create in Florida. Blown up and pinned to walls, the photos provided inspiration for the designers throughout the long life of the project.

More important, especially on the first trip, was seeing everything as a group, discussing the look, the feel, the experience. "Imagineers are storytellers," says Rohde, "and we knew we had to do more than just present animals. We had to make a story."

The team was struck by the "theme park-ness" of Africa. Truly wild places are just not accessible to the average tourist. Modern Kenya is a patchwork of farmlands and fenced grazing areas, and there were no game animals roaming free, except on ranches and preserves. Though these areas could be vast, they were fenced, hemmed in by agricultural areas. Even the nomadic Masai, whose cattle herds coexisted with wildebeests, zebras, and lions, lived on reserves. A simmering conflict between space for animals and space for people was palpable.

Left: the most talked-about moment of the Imagineers' initial African adventure occurred in Kenya at Lake Nakuru, a popular safari park. Word went out over the radios carried by drivers that a leopard had been seen. The information created a traffic jam. Forty or fifty vehicles converged on the tree where the leopard was perched, while dozens of tourists leaned out of windows to photograph an animal 300 feet away. "That's when we realized that the tourists' Africa is a theme park—just not a particularly well-run one," explains project writer Kevin Brown. "We knew the experience we could provide in the Animal Kingdom would be as good as or better than that."
Opposite: a thatched reception area of one safari lodge, woven around the trunk of an enormous baobab tree, became the inspiration for the African safari queue line.

THE AFRICA DIARIES

Team members took a total of six trips to Africa during the development of Disney's Animal Kingdom Theme Park. The artists and designers and writers kept journals of their thoughts and experiences. Many of the moments they recorded found their way into the African safari story.

" *The highlight of the trip was the hippos—big and strong and mean. One surged out of the water with a snort and chased our boat, mouth open. We boated slowly over stretches of water where tell-tale eddies betrayed hippos lurking beneath—lots of them. This evening was the first time I have felt the exhilaration I expected from Africa. Fifteen-foot crocodiles and massive hostile hippos crashed through the water. As sunset drew on, the animals became more aggressive. We rocketed along, skirting the primeval banks to find our way home.* **"**

JOE ROHDE, TEAM LEADER

" *We came upon a cloud of circling vultures—well over a hundred. They roosted shadowed in trees and swooped noisily in the understory. We traced the birds to the source of the commotion and found a dead juvenile elephant—VW van–size, with two-and-a-half foot tusks, seemingly not poached. Stomach eaten. Bad smell.* **"**

JOE ROHDE, TEAM LEADER

Aug 11, 1990. Masai Village—
Kenya.

The children, even though
with flies on their faces—
were happy, very well
behaved and very
curious. They had a
great time w/ Tony
and his video
camera, and they
loved me drawing
and my watercolor
set.
I'd like to paint
from photographs and
send it to them...

UMPANO.
cutest little boy.
(also photographed)

→ THREE DUDES AND A DHOW!

MY
LEFT
FOOT!

8/10
to NAKURU

66 I painted while we were
driving, desperate to capture
the beauty of this place—
standing up while the car was
moving, with my little portable
watercolor set, painting on the
run. Africa was the most gor-
geous place I'd ever seen. 99
ZOFIA KOSTYRKO,
SENIOR CONCEPT DESIGNER

21

66The land forms in the savannah are quite varied. Besides the kopjes, there are random grass-covered mounds, and we observed an interesting berm-like horizon similar in height to our surrounding berm. This ridge was unplanted, with only a smattering of trees in the foreground. It created a false horizon that would hide vehicles and buildings but still indicate a vast expanse beyond. This may be appropriate for our northern and/or western edges.99

JOHN SHIELDS,
LANDSCAPE PLANNER

66Smokey Africa saturates wanderlust. The Almighty's Great Rift, Masai-Mara, and spicy Zanzibar electrify imagination. Soaring sopranos and incessant buzzing over bellowing elephant vibrations: it's just nature's improvisational jazz. All the while, Joe's affinity for visualizing using originality and science opens a dreamworld of fascinating plants and geology.99

PAUL COMSTOCK,
LANDSCAPE ARCHITECT

SERENGETI
17 April 93

Leaving the lodge this morning we discovered a perfect wooden bridge to use for our rickety show bridge. We photo'd and video'd the heck out of it.

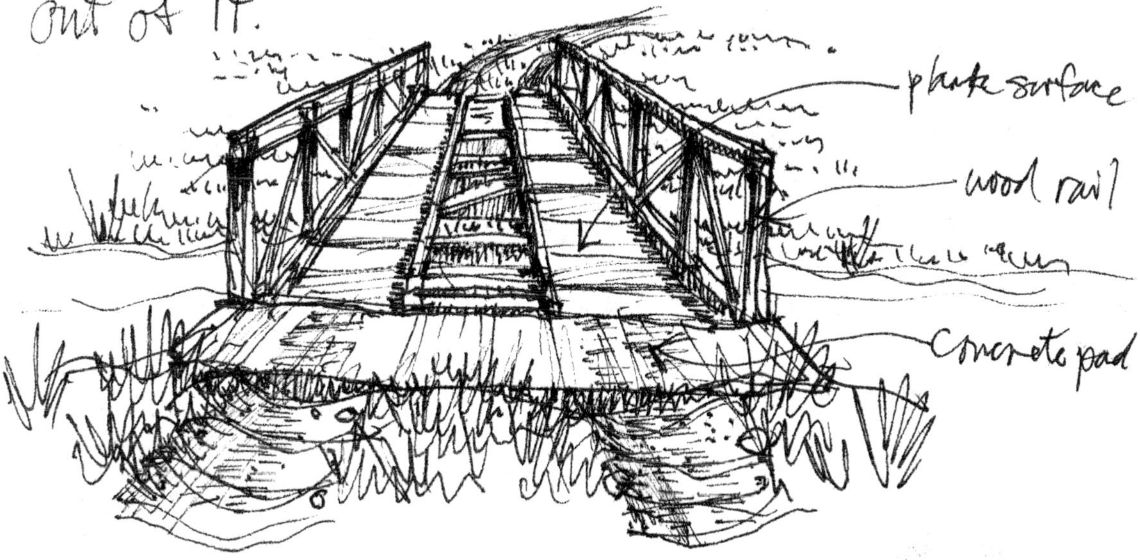

plank surface

wood rail

concrete pad

Soon we spotted a 2 cheetah just a bit off the road. After watching a while we noticed a baby Wildebeest 10ft behind from the 30,000 beast migration that he had crossed our path the night before. Before we knew it the cheetah slunk toward the baby and then darted toward it.

23

> **"**Over the phone, it sounded like a small project. I thought, 'It's got to be bigger than a petting zoo,' but I had no idea what they had in mind.**"**
>
> RICK BARONGI,
> ANIMAL CARE EXPERT

Rick Barongi, who consulted with the Imagineers on animal issues.

A FENCE AS HIGH AS AN ELEPHANT'S EYE . . .
(AIN'T NEARLY HIGH ENOUGH!)

Back home, the team got down to designing the safari. They needed an animal expert, someone who could reliably advise them on how to design both the "front of house"—habitats that the guests would see—and "back of house" facilities for animal care. Issues of grouping animals together, or seemingly together, needed to be addressed. How could the animals be encouraged to be active, to cluster in a picturesque and viewable valley, to interact? How high a fence could a particular antelope jump?

Bill Conway suggested the team contact Rick Barongi of the San Diego Zoo. Recently promoted from curator of the Children's Zoo to curator of mammals, Barongi was a trained zoologist with an interest in researching okapis, giraffes, and tapirs. "He was also," remembers Rohde, "an up-and-coming, forward-thinking guy. He was perfect for our team."

Patsy Tillisch invited Barongi to visit the team as a consultant, but told him very little about Disney Company plans.

The Imagineers, well informed in some areas, were weak in others. Barongi could help. Together, they talked about mixed herds of animals, how to get animals and guests close to one another, how to create better conditions for animals and more theming in their habitats. In sum, the Imagineers' visions could be realized. It all boiled down, Barongi explained, to acclimatizing animals to their conditions.

Designing for animals meant more than just worrying about fences or feeders.

Operations guru Eric Eberhart had to think through issues like maintenance early on: "What am I going to do when the collapsing bridge goes on the fritz and I have to send a maintenance worker to the crocodile river? Those aren't robots!"

YEAR TWO

In early 1991 Disney's Animal Kingdom Theme Park began to come together as artists created sketches, architects master-planned the park, and designers laid out rides. Using existing Disney attractions as their models, people crossed disciplines as each team member worked on a slate of proposed ideas.

The team had a "do first, ask later" attitude. Yet they always tried to design practically, with an eye to building the park.

EuroDisneyland was moving toward its 1992 opening, and the Walt Disney Company was in an expansive mode. The Imagineers needed, besides a high concept, some concrete definition for the Animal Kingdom project that would lay out how big the park would be, how many attractions it would have, how many guests would attend.

In spite of the project being green-lighted, experienced help was still hard to find. Operations' Eric Eberhart remembers one meeting on a ride design. Disney has a shorthand for rating rides and shows, derived from the days of A-, B-, C-, D-, and E-attraction tickets at Disneyland. An E attraction is the most exciting (think Space Mountain), while something like the King Arthur Carousel rates an A. Because "E-ticket" has entered American parlance to denote the best, it's reasonable to think everyone understands the system. Not so, says Eberhart. "Reviewing a design, I said, 'I think it's a D.' And this kid, a new designer eager to promote the ride, says, 'Oh no, it's better than that! It's at least a C!'"

TIGER, TIGER

As plans for the park progressed, Eisner challenged the Imagineering team. They were adamant about giving the guests a sense of "shared space" with wild animals, but Eisner wondered, "Are guests going to feel that animals are exciting enough?" As the design team caucused in their spartan warehouse, their rallying cry was, "Proximity equals excitement!" The plan that emerged was so audacious that the team dared not confide it even to Marty Sklar, Imagineering's creative leader.

Joe Rohde began the next meeting with corporate executives by squarely addressing the issue of animal encounters: "We know that there are concerns about whether animals are, in and of themselves, dramatic. The heart of the Animal Kingdom park is animals, and our guests' encounters with them. We have gone to great lengths to make sure that the animals will be displayed in a way that will bring them and people together as never before . . . "

The door to the room opened. A 400-pound female Bengal tiger, restrained by only a slender chain, stalked in. Rohde ignored the huge cat and kept talking as she prowled the room, coming within inches of Disney's key executives.

The effect on everyone present was palpable as the tiger, all rippling muscle and powerful claws, walked restlessly around the edges of the room. Disney president Frank Wells edged his chair closer to the table. Eisner stared. Sklar, kept in the dark by the team, gasped and looked at Rohde. It was, remembers one Imagineer, "a definite role reversal. Eisner and Wells confronted something so much more powerful than they were. They immediately saw the point of what we were trying to do in the park."

Twitching its whiskers, the tiger sat in the corner of the room, yawning, as Rohde continued, "Yes, there's an element of danger, but that's necessary for drama. Physical danger is an essential fact that animals deal with every day, and we want to drive that idea home . . ."

The tiger sauntered behind Rohde and was led out of the room as he concluded: "So you can see our position: proximity to animals— the illusion that they are right next to you—is essential."

The tiger gambit had helped the team make its point: live animals were an integral condition of the concept. Eisner and Wells capitulated. In the end, the presence of live animals was too powerful a dramatic tool to ignore.

EXPERTS ON ANIMALS

As the pace of design picked up, animal consultant Barongi was beginning to worry. He felt the team needed to hear the debate in the zoo community about animal care and containment issues. He called on a select group of colleagues from zoos around the country for a series of long, spirited meetings.

The consultants met with the Imagineers and argued—amicably—over almost everything. Mary Healy, curator of Disney's Discovery Island, was a member of the consultant team. She was impressed by the homework the Imagineers had done. "They knew the importance of the project, and they knew about the American Zoo and Aquarium Association and how to make contacts." Together, the group went over each animal proposed for the park and talked through everything related to both onstage and "backstage" areas.

The Imagineers wanted the onstage areas to appear as natural as possible. Unlike a zoo, Disney's Animal Kingdom park couldn't have vehicles interrupt the ongoing "show" to transport food, vet care, or animals. Animals had to seem close enough to touch but be safely removed from guests. Hidden barriers between predator and prey animals would have to be devised. The consultants diagrammed and debated placement and construction of pens, fences, moats, and ha-ha's, parallel ditches that form an invisible barrier.

A day was devoted to passive behavioral inducements for animals to stay in nice visual areas. The Imagineers needed help to figure out how to keep animals where they could be seen and enjoyed by guests. Consultants suggested disguising feeders: lions could congregate around a strategically placed feeder filled with catnip; birds could nip nectar from ports in fake flowers near walkways and benches.

Backstage got just as much attention. The animals' night houses would be equipped with heaters, movable walls, water, mud, and/or sun rooms. The experts talked about how many keepers and curators would be needed. They discussed vet facilities, including quarantine, nursery, and pathology; food preparation areas and equipment; even the strategy for dealing with animals that die (after a determination of cause of death, their bones could be donated to museums, or their eggs or sperm harvested for future use).

They developed a list of plants that would attract insects, which in turn would be food for or exist in symbiotic relationships with other animals. They discussed using fish for hippo waste management, a separate area for behavioral studies at Gorilla Falls, and soothing, piped-in music for the elephant barn.

FINDING A NICHE

At Imagineering's sprawling facilities in a Glendale industrial park, proximity to the central building, a former cosmetics factory at 1401 Flower Street, is coveted by many design teams and departments. While some prefer to labor away from the light of scrutiny, others like to be part of the action. When a team moves closer to the main lot, legitimacy is inferred, if not conferred. There are other benefits to being "on campus." Because design teams in a remote space can sometimes talk themselves into things, occasionally a fresh pair of eyes are good. Designers with more experience—none of the Animal Kingdom team members had ever designed a ride—might walk by and offer suggestions.

By the end of 1991, it was clear that the Animal Kingdom team was making progress in their drafty, remote building down the street from the main lot. The Imagineering workforce was shrinking as EuroDisneyland moved toward its spring opening. In January 1992 the team moved to a new set of offices on the Imagineering lot. They shared a corner of a former bowling alley previously converted to an office building (but with four lanes left intact for after-hours recreation). The cavernous space had room for the team to grow, if their park made headway.

In their new home, the team made an important presentation of the entire park to Walt Disney Company execs Eisner and Wells. Judson Green, president of Walt Disney Attractions, was there, and was transported by the idea. He remembers being "personally very excited. Seeing wildlife, exploring conservation themes—it's very powerful when we can find ways for kids to connect and participate." Green also saw the new park as positive for Disney employees. "Education, wildlife conservation, environmental protection, and community involvement are integral to the Disney culture. This is going to excite so many cast members," he recalls thinking. "It's a great fit."

Green's team was working on a concept for the Walt Disney World Resort of the future. That evolving philosophy held that Walt Disney World Resort is an incredible tourist destination, comparable to Las Vegas, or cruises, or Europe, or Asia, and that, as more diversity is built in, people will have more reasons to come back. Disney's Animal Kingdom Theme Park, even in its early form, promised to provide an adventure-filled, entertaining piece of the puzzle.

The skilled model builders at Imagineering created a 1/20th-scale view of the center of the park. Safari Village is in the foreground, with the Tree of Life in the upper right, and Harambe, the entrance to Africa, at the upper left. The model was used to study sight lines and as a sales tool that gave dimension to paintings and sketches.

IMAGINEERING A KINGDOM

66Like Walt was, Michael is very much in love with the creative process. He is a great motivator with a strong sense of what works with the public and what doesn't, of what's a good story. He builds on what we do.99

MARTY SKLAR,
VICE CHAIRMAN
AND PRINCIPAL CREATIVE
EXECUTIVE OF IMAGINEERING

The African safari was an integral part of Disney's Animal Kingdom™ Theme Park. To re-create the savannah, Imagineers planned a 100-acre attraction, larger than Disneyland® Park. Ominous smoking geysers introduce the adventure portion of the attraction.

Walt Disney Imagineering enjoys unusual access to Walt Disney Company CEO Michael Eisner, who has said he wishes his office was at Imagineering. His creative leadership is undisputed.

Midway through the design process, Eisner called a series of private brainstorming sessions with himself, Walt Disney Company president Frank Wells, and Imagineering's team for Disney's Animal Kingdom™ Theme Park. He told team members, "You've got to lead with your clichés! I want a dinoland, and I want it to be called DinoLand." Eisner identified areas and ideas he thought were weak. He pushed the team to be creative as they reconceptualized.

For two months, the team literally went back to the drawing board—in their case, the white display board that had been the focus of their initial work. New direction from Eisner meant that the park took on a new look, a new shape, and a new and sharper focus.

The Oasis was born, creating a total immersion in the world of animals and nature, starting at the entry gate. Another new idea—animals in the attraction queues and post-show areas—took shape.

The coalescing of "lands" around Safari Village began. The village moved to the center of the park, a departure point from which people went on adventures—safaris through Africa or DinoLand, U.S.A., fantasy journeys, or a trip behind the scenes to Conservation Station.

Senior concept designer Zofia Kostyrko credits architect Gerry Dunn with "a great leap forward"—Discovery River. Surrounding the classic Disney "hub" with water is "much more interesting" and gave the team the design freedom it needed.

BREAKING THROUGH

On April 6, 1992, the team came up with a plan that seemed to work. An entry garden would lead, via a bridge over a surrounding river, to a village spread out under the Tree of Life, at that time a walk-through attraction.

From the generic safari village, "ethnic" villages led to adventures in DinoLand, U.S.A., Africa, and Asia, and to places where fairy-tale and fantasy animals dwelled. The ethnic villages of Africa and Asia were real-world, modern re-creations. A train led from the river through outdoor safaris to a research station at the outer edge of the park. The river was akin to the railroad at the Magic Kingdom park. Most elements on that plan from 1992 are in place in the park today.

The team knew they had something. As the rest of the company celebrated the mid-April opening of EuroDisneyland, they waited impatiently to show their new ideas to team leader Joe Rohde, who was "truly amazed. The team had a great design, a real breakthrough. The only thing I added was the animal motif concept for Safari Village. We quickly agreed that was the park we wanted to do. From that point on, the park's conceptual program hasn't changed."

In summer 1992, the bowling alley offices began to fill up with concept architects Tom Sze and Ahmad Jafari, project manager Bob Pero, show designers Paul Torrigino and Dave Minichiello, show producers Ann Malmlund and Kelley Forde. As more players came on board, the project became real and urgent.

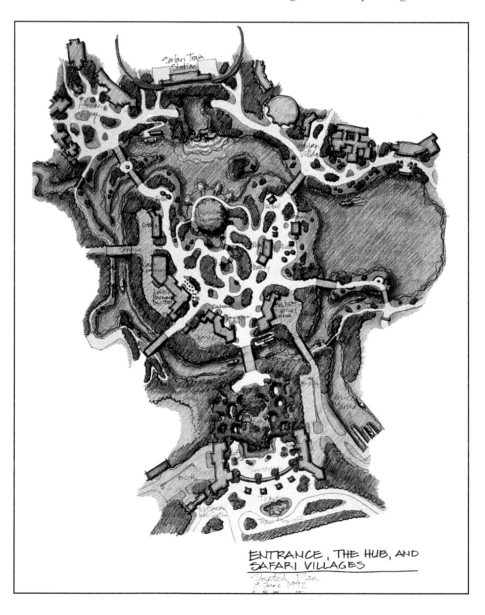

ENTRANCE, THE HUB, AND
SAFARI VILLAGES

Sketch Plan
9 June 1992

❝If you've been in the wild, surrounded by the foliage and flowers, you know you have to go over the top. We had to convince them that landscape was the show.❞

PAUL COMSTOCK,
LANDSCAPE ARCHITECT

This early layout of the center of the park shows the configuration of the Oasis (bottom), Safari Village and the Tree of Life (center), and the bridges to the safaris (top left and right). Wildlife Express, a train safari proposed for both Africa and Asia, is seen at top center.

REEN ACRES

The next design issue to crack was the sense of place that would be necessary to carry off the vast, natural-seeming vistas in the park. The team had traveled extensively to wild places, and "we knew there is no substitute for green," says landscape architect Paul Comstock.

Comstock grew up around plants at his father's wholesale nursery. The team asked him to bring in a few palms to flank the entrance to the conference room for their next meeting, a critical one for the landscape budget. So he did what came naturally: he borrowed more than a thousand plants from the family business, creating a leafy, flowering, 100-foot pathway leading from the bowling alley entrance to the meeting room. Mood lighting and a jungle sound track transformed the office into its own unique ecosystem.

"The whole building smelled different. It was real," recalls Zofia Kostyrko. "The air was fresher, and we all seemed more energetic. Every building should have a permanent jungle!"

More importantly, "we made the point," says Comstock. "We got the go-ahead for this immense, one-of-a-kind re-creation of an ecosystem. We got to create a world!"

ADVICE AND CONTENT

Animal specialist Rick Barongi was coming to Glendale regularly from the San Diego Zoo to brainstorm ideas and provide input on design. Architects from Seattle-based Jones and Jones, famous for its pioneering work in immersion exhibitry for zoos, had been hired to help Disney with design.

Barongi convened a final meeting with animal care consultants to tie down specifics of the safaris. What would it take to manage a large group of hippos? How big a space would be needed for elephants? Could elephants be bred? What about other things: barriers, plant interaction, animal interaction, back-of-house technology, the number of keepers that would be needed? The Imagineers opted for the highest standards, based on an overall philosophy of superior animal care and mindful of the huge volume of visitors expected at the park.

Meanwhile, a number of larger questions about exhibiting and caring for animals loomed.

Each year since 1991, the Imagineers had attended meetings of the American Zoo and Aquarium Association. Word that Disney was designing an animal park was an open secret among animal and conservation professionals. Michael Hutchins, the association's director of conservation and science, remembers, "I became worried about the park's connection with education and conservation."

At the meetings, Disney designers would get together with people like Karen Allen, then a public relations specialist at Conservation International. She reasoned that Disney, because of its power to tell stories, could be a real leader in the field. Allen thought the potential benefits were so huge it merited volunteering time to Disney.

That's exactly what Disney had in mind, on a much larger scale. Imagineering creative leader Marty Sklar felt that the company could not go forward with this large, unknown quantity—animals and conservation issues—without lots of high-level help. He asked Barongi to pull together a group of well-known zoo and conservation professionals who could help them on many levels, from formulating policy to reviewing design. The Advisory Board would hear about the park as it was being created and give feedback on its individual components as well as its overall mission. They could advise on animal rights and public relations issues as well as help the company make solid connections in the zoo community.

Barongi made up a list of colleagues—people who would give honest opinions, who wouldn't be afraid to speak up at meetings with Disney's highest-placed executives. He was putting in place "a link between the park and the natural world."

The 11-member board met for the first time in January 1993. A who's who of conservation, zoo, and zoology professionals, they spent three days reviewing designs, meeting Disney designers and executives, and talking.

Allen, from Conservation International, laid it on the line for Disney: "Every venue must have a conservation message. Your ethics have got to be impeccable, beyond reproach in terms of animal acquisition and access to information about how you run things."

Michael Hutchins recalls, "The Imagineers weren't animal professionals. They had no idea about some of the implications of their designs. Disney wanted to create fun. We helped them strike a balance between fun and education, between fun and conservation."

The advisers saw Disney's involvement in zoos and conservation as extremely positive. As Hutchins remarks, "What can Disney do for conservation? Disney can make it a household word. The public needs their emotional strings tugged but also needs to understand the details of the conservation story. If they don't care, it will all go away. Disney can make the emotional connection, the first step to intellectual commitment. After that comes action. A world without tigers and elephants? I wouldn't want to be there! And Disney has the power to inspire change."

Terry Maple of Zoo Atlanta says that being on the Advisory Board is one of the most important things he's done in his career. "The Disney Company, with its resources and ideas, would do things the zoo world couldn't do. Disney films, animation, and magazines can reinforce images through entertainment outreach. As long as Disney stays close to the truth of living animals in nature—if part of their story is always living creatures and how they're faring—they could turn the tide of conservation."

It was clear that the Advisory Board had a big idea for Disney: that the company should make some early, concrete contributions to conservation. This embryonic idea would become the Disney Wildlife Conservation Fund. Helping the conservation world with badly needed funding would help legitimize the project in the profession as well as with animal-rights activists, emphasizing, as Rick Barongi put it, that "we are not just displaying animals for entertainment. We have a real commitment to conservation and education."

> **Suppose everybody in the world is touched by this message five to ten years from opening day? This park could stimulate a new tide of conservation-mindedness and problem solving worldwide. I don't feel Disney should think anything else. This is a message of hope.**
>
> TERRY MAPLE,
> ADVISORY BOARD MEMBER

OLD FRIENDS, NEW JOBS

Bob Lamb runs a herd of Brangus cattle in central Florida. Through his day job, as general manager at Disney-MGM Studios in Florida, he learned about the proposal for Disney's Animal Kingdom Theme Park. "I heard all the objections—for example, even on slow days you have to feed the animals—but I thought it would be cool. There aren't that many themes for theme parks, and this was a very strong one."

Within a couple of months Lamb was the operations head of the fledgling park, splitting his time between California and Florida, where he still oversaw Disney-MGM Studios. His boss, Bruce Laval, knew that Lamb's long experience with the parks—starting as a tram driver in 1972, working with Imagineering during the design and opening of Epcot®—and his menagerie at home would make him the ideal person to shepherd the project through the next, crucial phase.

Running a theme park was second nature to Lamb, whose reputation at Disney-MGM Studios was for innovation and a hands-off approach to managing his staff. He put his best people in touch with Imagineering to continually refine the operational parameters of the park, and turned his attention to the animal part of his new domain.

Organizationally, the animal care staff of Disney's Animal Kingdom Theme Park would report to Lamb. He made it his business to begin to learn as much as he could about animals and conservation.

The Imagineering team attended the fall 1993 convention of the American Zoo and Aquarium Association. It was Lamb's first exposure to the zoo community, and "the longest week of my life," he says. He was introduced by the Imagineers and Barongi to "a flood of faces"—some of the most important people in the zoo world. Lamb recalls, "There was an amazing learning curve—on animals, conservation, animal activist organizations."

As Lamb contemplated what it would take to design the animal programs, he was more and more convinced that Rick Barongi was the right mix of visionary, entertainer, and hands-on zookeeper. "He fell into our laps, and we were smart enough to seize the moment," Lamb says.

In November, after a lot of negotiations and soul-searching, Barongi left the San Diego Zoo to become director of animal programs for Disney's Animal Kingdom Theme Park. "I was at a stage where zoos were changing too slowly. I had already directed the Children's Zoo at San Diego—and I saw this as a logical step for me." Most important, "Someone from the zoo community had to show a commitment. I thought from the animal side I could have a real impact. The fact that it was not guaranteed—that was a challenge for me."

And Disney encouraged him to keep up his outside research interests—a project on tapirs and training local biologists in Panama. Within weeks, Barongi was making his presence felt, setting the tone for everything animal-related that would follow.

Conservation Station was originally named Preservation Station. Barongi argued for a change. "With preservation, nothing happens. Everything remains as it was. But conservation is a proactive word. It implies making constructive moves and managing the inevitable, which is change. It's the catchword of the '90s; it's forward-looking."

Like what Disney's Animal Kingdom Theme Park would be.

Walt Disney Company CEO Michael Eisner felt the dinosaur safari lacked excitement. In the summer of 1993 he suggested using the budget to make an E ticket for DinoLand, U.S.A. The attraction would move indoors, becoming a jolting, lurching, thrilling dino encounter. Changing combinations of effects would ensure that guests never saw the same show twice. The Imagineers went back to their concept for DinoLand, U.S.A., itself—the conflict between chaos and order, authority and disobedience, youthful, creative minds vs. stodgy, controlling brains, and the park's overall theme of the weakness of technology in the face of nature—and began to work out the details for Countdown to Extinction.

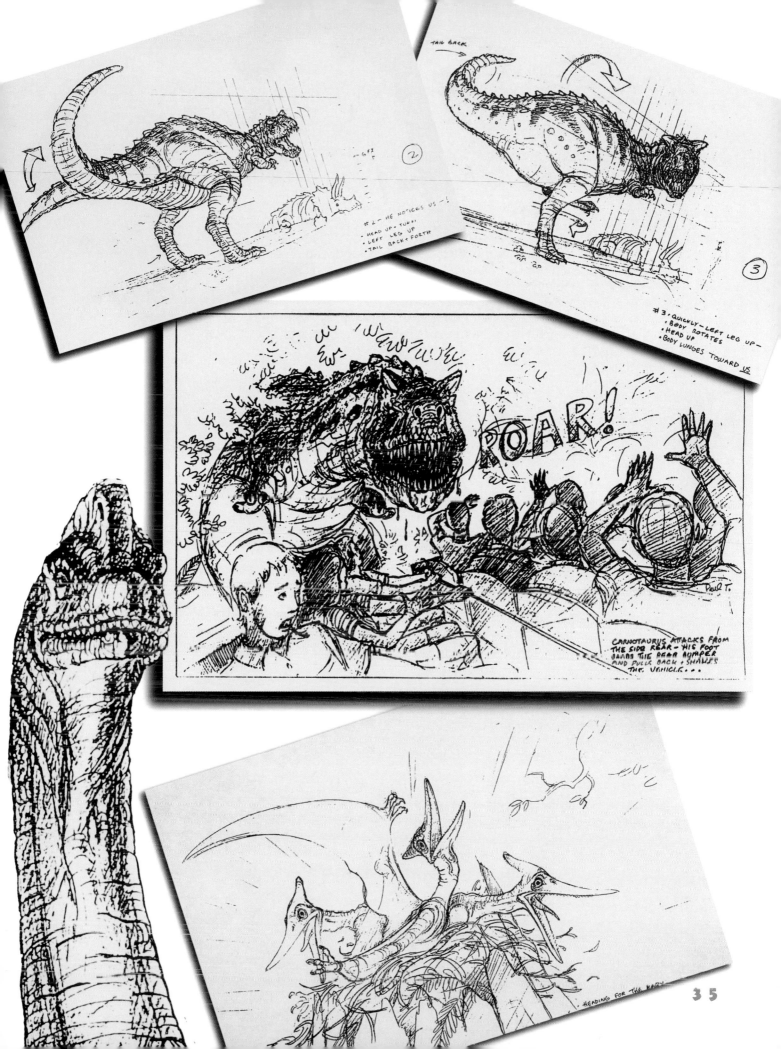

THE ARK SETS SAIL

By the fall of 1993, so many Imagineers and contractors were at work on the Animal Kingdom project that the offices were spread among the Imagineering lot and office buildings in Glendale and nearby Pasadena. Blueprints were being produced, ready to go to the bid process, as the design team was expanding, cranking out building layouts, ride tracks, facades, and set designs. Interiors were being tied down, props were being procured, scripts were being written, signs were being designed, and time and materials scheduled. Eric Eberhart was contacting

Operations colleagues on both coasts to get definition on everything from the size of queue areas and walkways to what should be included on a ride-control panel.

The scale models for the Tree of Life and Safari Village were taking up most of the cavernous Imagineering model shop; the team had to keep its large-scale African safari model in its own double conference room. The best way to view the models was to go to a second-story catwalk above the model-shop floor. Design teams were winging their way to Africa and Asia for research on buildings and vegetation, while interior designers sought out

Mexican artisans in remote villages to carve bats and weave kangaroo-shaped baskets for shops. Opening day was set for spring 1998.

When opening day is four and a half years away, the theme park design process becomes schizophrenic. The finish date is both far away and right around the corner. Set designs, paint finishes, figure movements, and live scripts can be adjusted until literally the last minute, but large-scale infrastructure, grading, and building layouts have to be tied down and lived with. Budget and "scope" are set. The horse trading among teams begins.

Imagineer Frank Newman suggested that the Tree of Life be made of deeply sculpted animal forms. Early concepts were more two-dimensional. Here, Newman creates the scale model of the park icon.

PLANNING TO BUILD

Before a Disney project is built, it exists in people's heads. While the minds of designers are occupied with story and set design, the brains of project and construction managers are sorting underground layers of utilities and listing relative priorities for the building of roads, buildings, and infrastructure.

A huge logistical undertaking like a theme park can't be built all at once, even if enough workers could be found. Just providing parking and lay-down (preparation) yards for dozens of contractors—who brought in heavy equipment, office trailers, and squadrons of laborers and craftspeople—required another contractor to create a huge concrete pad. Imagineers decided the contractors' parking lot would ultimately serve as the parking lot for guests.

Planning the construction of Disney's Animal Kingdom Theme Park fell to an elite team of managers and planners. Project manager Bob Pero, construction managers Scott Williams and Jerre Kirk, and planning director Frank Addeman began thinking about the park's building sequence in 1992.

The designers asked the planners for two growing seasons on the park's African savannah before the animals would arrive in fall 1997. That meant that all the plants would have to be installed by spring 1996. And that meant that the underground utilities (about 60 miles worth) would have to be installed, the land sculpted (to the tune of more than 4 million cubic yards of earth moved), and the rockwork (a million square feet of the stuff) installed before plant-

ing could begin. "It sounded so simple," laughs Williams, "until we started digging into the details. We realized we'd need four to five hundred people just to build the rocks. It would take a year to build the concrete baobab trees. We'd need seventeen pipe crews, working all at once on some days. We thought, we'd better get to work on the site *now!*"

The planners utilized bar charts, schedules, index cards pinned to the walls, and years of experience in the Disney corporation and outside, on projects as diverse as nuclear power plants, big-city high-rises, and the Aquarium of the Americas. "We are all neatniks," admits project vice president Jack Blitch. "Our offices are well organized. We like to make lists and think things out in a logical sequence."

Would constructing the huge Countdown to Extinction facility first "lock out" the ability to build the rest of DinoLand, U.S.A.? Could all the "cut" from dredging Discovery River make up the "fill" or relief needed to sculpt the African savannah? When did the animal houses need to be finished in order to accommodate the earliest arrivals at the park? What were the critical milestones—in every land, in every building—that had to be met in order to open the park on schedule and on budget?

Early in the design process the strategy was settled: bid out the work in discrete, coordinated packages to general contractors around the country who would bring their skilled personnel to Florida. At its peak, the park would employ 2,600 construction workers in a single day.

IMAGINEERING A TREE

In concept, the Tree of Life was a fabulous idea—a soaring tribute to the interconnectedness of life. But as the design process evolved, the natural appearance of the tree was becoming sublimated—and almost eliminated—by serious structural and engineering concerns. For an enormous structure like this to be affordable, it would need to be assembled from prefabricated components. And to make a nearly 140-foot "tree" stand up to hurricane-force winds in excess of 74 mph suggested that the branches would have to be stylized, stiff, and regular.

Mitch Gill, manager of artificial foliage at Imagineering, got an early look at plans for the tree for which his department would supply more than 100,000 leaves. Gill, who has a background in theater, looked at the plans and realized that when the leaves were struck by sunlight, the rigid internal structure of the branches—evenly spaced hexagons on 10-foot legs—would be revealed. It would look more like a geodesic dome than a majestic tree.

Gill knew that the team's goal was to make the tree as natural-looking as possible. His department had set up a development program with Imagineering's Research and Development division to explore new materials. Some of that money was earmarked for the Tree of Life, and the team—Michael Brown, Les Skoloda, and Russ Moody—explored making limbs not of steel, but of a kind of structural, flexible, injection-molded fiberglass. The branches would socket on to the steel base of the tree, and taper from a 2-foot circumference at the base to 2 inches where the leaves were attached.

Now the question was how to design the branches so that they would appear natural, random, and lifelike. Each one could have been sculpted individually, but the cost would have been astronomical. The branches would have to be mass-produced. Gill proposed that he use two weeks and a new computer program to study the problem. The program allowed him to create renderings, animate them, rotate them, even "fly around" them.

After constructing a model, Gill calculated that to cover the entire tree canopy he would need 32 balls, each 24 feet in diameter. Each ball would have two types of secondary branches that hooked to two types of tertiary branches. These four types of branches could be randomly assembled, turned, and adjusted to create natural shapes as they tapered to the end branches and out to the leaves. "It was a lot like following the dots: the leg-bone connected to the ankle bone," Gill explains. "The computer proved that this could be done in theory, with a certain number of branches. It would cost the same as the dome, but instead it would look like a tree."

In concept, they'd proved it. Imagineers made a preliminary model to test the theory. Some branches were sacrificed in the reshaping of the tree to make it even more lifelike. Soon sculptors were hard at work on the scale model, shaping the trunk into swirling animal forms.

As the Tree of Life stands in the park today, 45 secondary branches lead to 756 tertiary branches that in turn taper to 7,891 end branches. A staggering 102,583 green leaves—each more than a foot long, fabricated of a

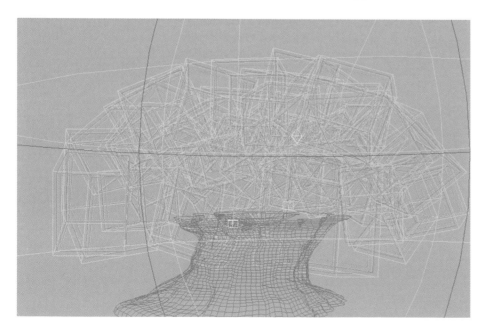

Opposite, far left: a computer "wire frame" rendering of the Tree of Life began to suggest a solution to a too-rigid structure.
Opposite, near left, top: the wire frame of a single branch, including secondary, tertiary, and end branches; bottom: the branch fully rendered on the computer.
This page, clockwise from top: the base branches await sculptors; a near-finished branch, showing the various textures; a finished branch, hung from a crane that will plug it into the trunk.

Even the storyboards for the African safari were unique. (Above: a road in the forest; below: Hippo River.) Instead of using a series of typical movie screen–proportioned sketches, show designers created "rollouts" that indicated left, right, and forward views simultaneously. To see the effect, put your nose in the fold of these pages while holding the illustrations at eye level. The scenes imagined by the team in two dimensions can be seen in three dimensions on the savannah today.

special plastic called Kynar—are the tree's crowning glory.

Using the original computer printouts as a guide, the team assembled the branches on the ground, away from the massive trunk of the Tree of Life. The branches were then carried over and plugged in by a crane. The canopy of the giant icon went together on-site like an oversized construction toy.

IMAGINEERING AFRICA

A unique attraction unparalleled in Disney history, the African safari was riddled with challenges beyond the most obvious one of including live animals. The first question the Imagineers answered was, "Why is this not a zoo?" The answer: the safari had a theme; it addressed the conflict between humans and the natural world. It would be a dramatic, interactive adventure story woven around animal encounters in a beautiful, natural setting.

Research trips to Africa had resulted in some hair-raising moments as well as confrontation with serious issues in conservation. In Harambe, the created village that would lead to the safari adventure, it would be clear that the savannah was managed by the townspeople and that poachers were threatening the ecosystem—and everyone's livelihood. With that setup, guests could

become part of an effort to thwart a gang of ivory poachers. The guests would see magnificent animals in an authentic setting, then join in a chase to prevent the poaching of an elephant matriarch.

SOOO BIG

The next nut to crack was the size of the safari itself. For the team of Imagineers, the answer became, "How big *can* it be?" They used an exercise to show each other what they hoped to achieve with the big vistas of the savannah. A four-block stretch of lightly traveled city street stretches behind the Imagineering main lot. The designers, standing at one end of the street, pointed out a small truck parked at the other end. "That truck is the size of an elephant. From here, it looks as big as a peppercorn. That is what we want. That is the scale we are talking about."

The size was finally settled on: about 100 acres, an unprecedented area for what would essentially be a stage set. And the set design for the savannah had to accomplish many things in addition to telling the story. Landscape designers and civil engineers had to collaborate to hide necessary buildings—both animal back-of-house areas and attractions in other lands that might be visible. Disney's Animal Kingdom Theme

Park also had to hang together as a place, with rivers and ridgelines making geologic sense so that guests would, as they might when attending a play, "willingly suspend disbelief" and become involved in the story.

FROM TINY ACORNS . . .

With the bones of the safari in place, it was time for the landscaping team to "decorate" the set, an area larger than many of Disney's existing theme parks. The landscaping would not only be extensive, covering every surface; it also had to be authentic-looking and seem mature. A plan to conserve native oak trees and give them acacia-looking "crew cuts" was one early landscaping breakthrough. Transfers from the Disney tree farm were supplemented, in time-honored Disney tradition, with purchases of unwanted plants from people's backyards and sites slated for development, and through the nurseryman's grapevine.

Then the landscapers came up with an "early acquisition" proposal. They asked for money to buy small plants early (and more cheaply) and grow them on the property. "Accelerators"—pots of pierced, corrugated tin—helped twigs grow into trees in just two years. Outside growers propagated the millions of grass shoots needed to cover the savannah.

The most important point in the landscapers' program was asking for two years of growing time, once the plants were in the ground, so that they would be well established on opening day. With the essential cooperation of financial planners who understood the wisdom of spending a little early to get a lot later, the far-sighted landscape design team began to create their masterpiece.

CAUTION: IMAGINEERS ON BOARD

Early on, the Animal Kingdom design team pictured the African safari traveled by small vehicles that would give guests the illusion of traveling with their family alone on the vast plains. But to accommodate anticipated guest demand, the vehicles proliferated. Imagineers decided that they wanted to avoid the "traffic jam" look that had disappointed them on their own trips to Africa, so the safari vehicle grew in size. This solution kept the vistas pure, with the compromise that guests would travel in somewhat larger groups.

Rather than having vehicles run on a track, with programmed encounters along the route, the designers searched for a way for safari vehicles to hit plot points and keep moving while preserving interaction with birds and free-roaming hoofed animals that

could cross in front of guests. The Imagineers created a vehicle that would be driven by a ride operator. It would travel over a permanent road complete with washed-out bridges engineered to provide the requisite bumps and thrills.

A test vehicle was built and a small portion of the ride track was laid down in an Imagineering parking lot. Imagineering creative leader Marty Sklar rode in the prototype, coffee cup in hand. The carefully orchestrated jolts and bumps were pronounced authentic and believable as his coffee spilled all over him and his fellow passengers.

NIGHT LIGHTS

Operations wanted to be able to run the African safari at night during times of peak demand. This request represented a major challenge, since the cost of lighting 100 acres even for only a few weeks a year was prohibitive.

Lighting designer Dave Taylor tried a variety of ideas, finally deciding to use mounted search-lights and a series of "smart lights" that, when signaled by the vehicle's passage, subtly illuminate selected animal enclosures. "Moonlight" on the savannah, plus the headlights, tail-lights, and campfires of the poachers, "sweeten" crucial scenes so that the safari story gets told on even the darkest winter night.

RUMORS FLY

By March 1995, rumors of final approval for the Animal Kingdom project were circulating around Imagineering. Jack Blitch, fresh from the completion of Blizzard Beach water park, formally joined the growing team as project vice president. Blitch had taken part in an expansion of Disney-MGM Studios—the Twilight Zone Tower of Terror™ attraction and Sunset Boulevard—that had eight project managers and two show producers. Disney's Animal Kingdom had only three project managers and three show producers. The leanness of the new team conferred several advantages; the group was "extremely well-managed, with lots of team ownership and quick communication. We were able to make decisions on the fly."

A poster was created and printed. In great secrecy, a June media announcement was planned. The Advisory Board was dispatched to Florida. The Tree of Life model was crated and shipped. Not even the core team was let in on the secret, but, says writer Kevin Brown, "It was obvious. Suddenly all speculation came to a halt."

By 10 a.m. on June 21 the official announcement was in full swing, complete with African dancers, the Advisory Board, and a stage full of Disney executives. Michael Eisner picked up the thread of the team's first creative ideas when he described the park as "based on mankind's enduring love for animals and celebrating all animals that ever or never existed."

A curtain rose to reveal the spectacular model of the Tree of Life. Flanked by paintings, a preview video and poster featuring dinosaurs, a dragon, and a safari vehicle perched on a rickety bridge, company officials and board members explained Disney's fourth theme park.

"This is to the traditional zoo as the motion picture was to the stage play," said Eisner, "a leap forward that keeps the concept of combining education and entertainment alive and well. The need for awareness of endangered animals and their environments has never been greater. We are in a unique position to promote a deeper understanding and love for all animals."

Green reflected the euphoria among the staff: "We believe the Animal Kingdom is a great investment—great for Walt Disney World, and a great platform for all divisions. And we've been reaching out to the conservation world. They believe we can reach millions and millions of people."

Vice chairman of the board Roy E. Disney was there. Recalling the rise in interest in banning DDT after a well-received program on falcons appeared on Disney's *The Wonderful World of Color*, he concurred, "We do make a difference if we do it right. It's been our tradition all along. We've done more than anybody in the world except Jacques Cousteau to sensitize people to the needs of the planet."

Back at Imagineering there was elation, adulation, and frantic activity. Jack Blitch recalls the fallout: "Everyone realized, 'It's a real project!'" Bids on contracts came in on or under budget. The earth-moving for Disney's Animal Kingdom Theme Park began in August. With opening day set for spring 1998, a mere two-and-a-half years remained to build Disney's largest-ever theme park.

Left: Disney executives (from left to right) Roy E. Disney, Al Weiss, Judson Green, Michael Eisner, and Rick Barongi enjoy a remark by Joe Rohde at the media announcement. Opposite: over 4 million cubic yards of dirt were moved on the huge site of Disney's Animal Kingdom Theme Park. Sculpting a rolling landscape from virtually flat ground took years of planning and execution.

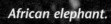
African elephant.

ANIMAL HOUSE

66 *The way we are presenting animals to the public is unique. I firmly believe that if people are having a good time they are willing to listen to you. This is a medium that can help in the long run for the conservation of the Earth. That this company can put so many resources into the message is incredible. We have a vision, and the whole team shares it. We look farther down the road than right now.* **99**

BRUCE READ,
GENERAL CURATOR

Which animals? Where would they be seen? How would they be housed? Where would they come from? Who would care for them? As Disney's Animal Kingdom™ Theme Park became a reality, Rick Barongi went to work to identify the future stars of the park—critters comely and curious, the ambassadors that would tell the stories of their species to the world.

Working with the designers almost since the park's inception, Barongi had helped create lists of animals for each land. He would act as the reality check to the conceptual ideals of the planners at Walt Disney Imagineering. A thundering herd of wildebeests became a group of 10, based on the space available. When the species and the number of animals were agreed upon, the homes for the animals would be designed.

Barongi relied on his extensive contacts in the zoo world, developed through his 25-year career, to help him advise the Imagineers. The Advisory Board convened formally, and its members were contacted individually about certain animals: How active will they be in Florida's heat? How will we get them in at night? How will we protect the vegetation? Would birds hop the moats and get in with the predators? Gemsboks are very beautiful animals—majestic southern African antelopes—but their aggressive nature made them poor candidates for both sides of the savannah; they would have fought with antelopes already slated to live there.

Avian expert Grenville Roles recalls creating a list of birds of the African savannah by height and weight. "I understood the height—they wanted to know if they could be seen from the vehicle—but weight?" To develop the list, he created a range of species for a certain

> **66Live animals are dynamic, sensitive, and emotional. They compel us to learn.99**
>
> *BETH STEVENS,*
> *CONSERVATION AND*
> *SCIENCE DIRECTOR*

habitat out of his reference books. He worried about heat and humidity tolerance, about how the birds would respond to stresses like a vehicle lumbering along every minute or so, and about whether they are delicate or hardy. Taxon Advisory Groups, Species Survival Plans, and fauna groups all have keeping and breeding recommendations that he took into account. He checked into the availability of birds from captive-breeders. "This all coalesces, and then it boils down to what the curator likes."

Animals in zoos become available to other institutions in a

variety of ways, mostly through success in breeding, but "responsible zoos have space to house their excess collection," says Barongi. Everyone cares where their animals go. Animal dealers have to be respectable middlemen with good facilities. No curators want their animals to end up on hunting ranches.

Zari, the first female giraffe in the collection, is a good example of the sometimes serendipitous way that animals have come to Disney's Animal Kingdom Theme Park. The Portland Zoo had an offer for Zari from an animal dealer. General curator Dennis

Below: female nyala; opposite: reticulated giraffes.

PERMIT ME

Cooperation between Disney's Animal Kingdom personnel and the governing agencies was essential. The park had to be licensed as an institution that can keep animals and display them to the public. The back-of-house areas were completed well before the occupants were due to arrive, so federal and state officials could inspect the areas. On-site visits covered facilities, forage, and systems for dealing with water and manure. The inspectors looked for proper shade in the habitats as well as the availability of drinking water in the animals' houses.

Florida agencies grant the licenses to bring animals into the state and to exhibit them. The U.S. Department of Agriculture grants licenses to hold and display mammals. The U.S. Department of the Interior granted a permit that allowed the park to acquire captive-bred, non-native threatened and endangered wildlife. Curators and registrar Lynn McDuffie compiled the paperwork to satisfy all permit requirements, and the animal care staff worked with the Imagineering team and Operations to make sure all physical requirements were met.

Pate called Barongi to ask if he had room for her. At the time he didn't, but she had excellent bloodlines, so Barongi said they'd take her: "She'll breed in '98 and maybe have a calf in '99, after a fourteen-month gestation."

Ultimately, some of the creatures now residing at Disney's Animal Kingdom Theme Park were purchased. Some were sent on loan, some were donated. The amount of money that changed hands was "minimal," according to Barongi. "The cost of transporting the animals to the park was more than the cost of the animals in almost every case." For animals on loan, the arrangement is often that Disney will donate half their offspring to the lending institution.

Below: red kangaroo; opposite: white rhinoceros calf.

PLAYING BY THE RULES

From the beginning, Disney's Animal Kingdom Theme Park was dedicated to two propositions: its animals would come from captive-bred populations whenever possible, and it would attempt to work at all times within the zoo profession's Species Survival Plans and Taxon Advisory Groups.

"No animal will be acquired if it is to the detriment of the wild population of the species," emphasizes Barongi. Perhaps the park will take animals out of the wild one day, but only if they are doomed in the wild: if their habitat has been destroyed, or if they would be shot—for instance, when parks and refuges in Africa run out of room and need to "cull" their animals. "The key," says Barongi, "is that we have to get our credibility established before we accept wild animals."

For instance, Imagineers originally planned to have giant otters at the park but were told they would have to catch them in the wild. Instead, the park is now involved with giant otter conservation in the field. Meanwhile the Tree of Life will house captive-born Asian small-clawed otters.

"Nature's not a peaceful, beautiful place," says Barongi, whose field work has taken him to South America and Africa. "If we could interview the elephants from an African preserve where they will be killed because there's no range left, and ask them if they'd like to live on six acres in Florida or have their family destroyed, I think we'd hear they'd rather come here. So we want to leave ourselves the option to rescue animals when necessary.

"We can't be so politically correct that we avoid taking on battles on behalf of the animals. We can't make a blanket statement that we will never, under any circumstances, take animals out of the wild, because that might be harmful to long-term animal conservation too."

The American Zoo and Aquarium Association breeding recommendations help Disney's Animal Kingdom Theme Park obtain well-bred animals using a compendium of who is breeding animals, who can breed animals, who should breed animals. Three-quarters of Animal Kingdom mammal species have Species Survival Plans—all the primates, lions, okapis, and giraffes, as well as storks, macaws, parrots, and African flamingoes.

MAKING HABITATS MORE THAN HABITABLE

As the list of animals grew more concrete, so did the park documents. Barongi worked with the show producers, as well as Jones and Jones consultants Duane Dietz, Jim Brighton, and Pat Janikowski. They were the point men reviewing final designs for the "onstage" habitats—the shade trees and moats, ha-ha's (double ditches) and turnbacks and sheer walls that would keep the animals in their onstage paddocks and in sight of the guests. The "back of house" areas—the animals' night houses and barns, offstage paddocks and pools—got extra scrutiny. Because of the consultants' experience building animal habitats all over the world and Barongi's hands-on work as a keeper and a curator, they were a formidable team. Janikowski can call out specs from his head on primate-proof hinges, nontoxic paint, and the strength of steel beams, while Barongi talks about protected contact, or introduction techniques, or where the keepers would like to have their offices. Brighton and Dietz consulted with the Imagineers about types of plants the animals were likely to eat or trample, and how to protect vital shade trees from hungry ungulates.

The blueprints were reviewed at 30, 60, and 100 percent completion. Barongi made a lot of phone calls to zoo colleagues in the several months between the reviews, requesting changes based on new information. Since they were being built from the ground up, these habitats could be state-of-the-art, reflecting the latest thinking in the zoological field.

When (inevitably) the budget was cut, Barongi's philosophy was to take out an entire concept, "rather than nickel-and-diming habitats. We lost hyenas and wild dogs on the African safari due to budget. But I didn't want to make compromises across the board."

The biggest challenge was dealing with animal enclosures in the park's central region and south end. These onstage habitats for small mammals and birds will have millions of visitors each year, and curators wanted the animals to be able to hide when they need a break. Back-of-house areas were difficult to conceal. Some were placed in plain sight and disguised; the stone lemur house near the Tree of Life is "camouflaged" as a Safari Village building.

The strategy was to let the lush habitat plantings grow for two long Florida seasons, giving the vegetation a fighting chance to withstand the nibbling, prancing, lumbering, pawing creatures that eventually would call them home. To meet everyone's criteria, the park's onstage animal areas had to be finished by fall 1997 in order to open with the animals in place in spring 1998.

As plans for the park came together, the team realized that animals acquired before fall 1997 would have to be housed off-site. Every one of the thousand-plus animals would have to undergo state-mandated (or more stringent Disney mandated) quarantine, and become acclimated to

> **If someday you do opt to take an animal out of the wild, you explain why. That's what Disney's Animal Kingdom park can do—present the facts, so our guests understand the issues.**
>
> RICK BARONGI,
> DIRECTOR OF
> ANIMAL PROGRAMS

Florida's humid climate. Curator Mary Healy volunteered the use of Discovery Island for incoming bird species like flamingoes, East African crowned cranes, demoiselle cranes, roseate spoonbills, and hammerkopfs. Some of the offspring of the 300-strong scarlet ibis flock, the world's largest, would also come to Disney's Animal Kingdom Theme Park from their former home on Discovery Island.

Some zoos were able to keep the animals promised to the Animal Kingdom park until the facilities were completed. But Disney had to arrange housing for some 200 animals at a private institution in Florida while the park was readied for its residents.

LOOKING FOR PEOPLE

As Disney's Animal Kingdom Theme Park was being built and the animal collection assembled, Barongi was building the animal care staff. He started to recruit a general curator as soon as the park was announced. He knew he wanted to hire Bruce Read, a well-respected expert from the St. Louis Zoo. He was the only person with construction background, solid scientific credentials, and hands-on animal experience. Barongi began a full-court press to get his man.

Bruce Read came to the Animal Kingdom project in 1996, after spending his entire working life at the St. Louis Zoo. He was born across from the zoo and raised in Dogtown. As a kid he raised boxers and confesses, "I liked animals better than people." After graduating from the University of Missouri with a degree in animal husbandry, he had a choice of going to work at Ralston Purina or at the St. Louis Zoo as a keeper. "I had to wear a tie at Purina, so I chose the zoo," laughs Read, who

PART OF A DREAM

Joining a project like Disney's Animal Kingdom Theme Park is a once-in-a-lifetime proposition. Rarely is an animal facility built from the ground up with so much time, effort, monetary investment, and expertise. And rarely does one come along with so much potential. Staffers are passionate about what the Disney park can do for the animal kingdom as a whole.

Bird curator Grenville Roles says, "We can be creation-significant, not just show and financially significant. That's the ultimate justification for our existence, as people individually and as a park."

For general curator Bruce Read, it's a dream come true. "The Animal Kingdom offers me the opportunity to actually establish what I've preached for twenty years. We've built an organization with solid partners to institute the scientific management of a zoo collection and help, by example, to show good long-term management. As a team starting from scratch, we can lay a foundation for a park in which guests have a great time seeing the animals, and manage it so that it's beneficial for the collection and the individual species.

"The blending of these two professions—entertainment and displaying animals—is extraordinary. These two professions belong together. Entertainment will help conservation in the long run. It's where we should be in the zoo profession. I'm grateful to be here."

prefers Animal Kingdom logo shirts in a comfortable cotton knit as his work attire.

In Read's nearly 25 years at the St. Louis Zoo, things got increasingly codified, written down, and more scientific. It was a trend in the field that he spearheaded at his institution. When he began his career, zoos relied on oral tradition and mentoring. But Read had been trained in the science of animal husbandry.

"My whole career has been promoting the scientific management of zoo animals," Read says. In 1974 he bought his first computer for keeping records about birth and death, acquisition, shipping and transfers, behavior and veterinary problems, and other projects. All this accurate record-keeping later fed into the American Zoo and Aquarium Association programs for planned breeding, like Species Survival Plans and studbooks, and resulted in increased success with captive breeding and a host of other conservation issues that have since pervaded the zoo community.

Read sees Disney's Animal Kingdom Theme Park both as an important player in the zoo profession and as a powerful advocate for animals. "The potential of what we have is amazing. The opportunity to start from scratch with the scientific management of animals—it's the basis of what we're doing. As we change from an oral to a written tradition, hopefully this transition will raise zoos to a whole new level."

It is Dr. Beth Stevens' job to "look farther down the road." As the conservation and science director for Disney's Animal Kingdom Theme Park, part of her position description is to "seize inspirational moments in the park." She deals with both the public and zoo professionals. "We're creating the science of animal management because we have to, and we'll disseminate it. It will be a major contribution to the captive-animal community."

In terms of working with guests, the most intensive opportunities will be at Conservation Station, Gorilla Falls Exploration Trail, and DinoLand, U.S.A. Cast members in those locations will be trained by the conservation and education staff. Like docents at a zoo, they'll be able to talk about everything on view. "These staff members will be people who live and breathe Disney's Animal Kingdom," promises Stevens.

"The classroom is the park," says Stevens, and the lessons are about conservation and respect: "the appreciation of wildlife and wild places, understanding our place in the circle of life, realizing that the natural environment has value to our everyday lives."

Like many staff members at Disney's Animal Kingdom Theme Park, Stevens conducts ongoing research with which she'll remain active. In 1996, she fitted wood storks outside Savannah, Georgia, with transmitters, 60 grams in weight, "a little backpack." The packs broadcast to a satellite that records migratory information and is hooked up to an Internet site so that anybody can track these birds. The design of the project exemplifies how Stevens sees her role: as a committed conservation biologist sharing her findings with the world. The philosophy behind her field work is the philosophy behind her job at Disney's Animal Kingdom Theme Park. "We'll get guests involved with things we do on an everyday basis. If we make science a part of education, the science will benefit."

> **66If ultimately we can make a difference in one—or numerous—species or habitats, that will validate our lives.99**
>
> GRENVILLE ROLES,
> CURATOR OF BIRDS

Opposite: cheetah; above: cotton-top tamarins.

FOR THE BIRDS

The first curator—a species of super-keeper in charge of the collection, the personnel, and the management of the animals and their habitats—at Disney's Animal Kingdom Theme Park was Grenville Roles, curator of birds. Welsh by birth and international by experience, Roles has an incredible passion for birds, which he characterizes poetically as "buoyant, luminous" (parrots), "jewel-like and mellifluous" (pittas), and "helpless, dewy-eyed" (ostrich chicks). A consultant early on in the design phase, Roles came from the Tracy Aviary in Salt Lake City. He got his start as a $3-a-week keeper charged with recording minutiae about pheasants at Gerald Durrell's zoo on the Isle of Jersey.

Ninety-five percent of the birds at Disney's Animal Kingdom Theme Park will be captive-born and -bred. A committed conservationist, Roles is careful about the sources of his birds. His most precious experiences have been in the wild, observing behavior, and he thinks the Animal Kingdom park can re-create that feeling for the guests. "This is a window on the natural world. It should be breathtakingly elegant, a visitation. We want to inspire awe. We are sharing the same air, same space, same sun with these magnificent creatures."

Roles brims with stories about birds. The hoopoe, an African bird, makes a call that sounds like its Latin name, *Upupa epops*. One of the few wild-caught birds in the collection is the kori bustard, a large, terrestrial crane relative

Above: ostrich; right: East African crowned crane; opposite: male lowland gorilla.

from Africa. Roles promises that its impressive displays—"tail cocked, pendulous throat pouch waggling, wings spread, stamping its weirdly disproportionately small toes, coupled with deep growls and roaring calls often likened to those of lions—will be magnificent. We know so little about them that it is an important species for us to study."

The biggest challenge is keeping birds on the savannah and in view of the guests. They will be pinioned so that they can't fly out of the park, but that limits their natural response to predators—to take to the air. Guinea fowl, spotted, chicken-size birds, make lots of noise and employ a group defense, but others must flee on the ground to protected refuge areas that Roles hopes will prove effective day after day.

He good-naturedly but heartily dislikes ostriches, of which there will be 20 on the savannah. "Disgusting birds," he laughs. "Rick Barongi chose them before I got here. They will eat anything. One that died in Salt Lake had underwear, socks, spoons, and a dog collar in its stomach." Yet even ostriches excite his curiosity. On the savannah, austral and red-necked ostriches will be mixed, though they live separately in the wild. "Will they socialize? How will they use the habitat, and how will they interact with the hoofed animals?" he wonders.

The first five years will be spent learning, Roles thinks. It will be an experimental, study phase to find out how to best utilize all the facilities for the good of the animals at Disney's Animal Kingdom Theme Park, and ultimately in the wild.

> **"It's not easy listening for an antelope's heartbeat when it's kicking out the light above your head."**
> — PEREGRINE WOLFF,
> VETERINARY SERVICES DIRECTOR

SAY "HEE-AAH"

The health of the animals at Disney's Animal Kingdom Theme Park is assured through a complex protocol that begins with a quarantine when they arrive. For 30 days they are closely observed and a baseline physical evaluation is developed. It's just the beginning of the "awesome animal care" envisioned by Rick Barongi, Bruce Read, and Bob Lamb when they hired veterinary services director Dr. Peregrine Wolff, who oversees a staff of four vets.

Seven days a week, the vets arrive before dawn, read reports from keepers and zoological managers, then inspect and evaluate animals that may not be able to go "onstage." From 5:00 to 7:00 a.m. they perform any early-morning procedures on animals slated to go out to the habitats.

For the vet staff it works out to caring for about 800 animals each, since they also care for 80 horses at Walt Disney World® Resort and the other animals at the Tri-Circle D Ranch, Discovery Island (800 birds, mammals, and reptiles), Typhoon Lagoon, and The Living Seas at Epcot® (about 1,500 fish, plus turtles, dolphins, and manatees).

Every animal is a unique challenge, say the vets. "Primates and big cats really get to know you," says Wolff. "I could walk into the cat house at Lincoln Park Zoo, where I was a vet, in a crowd of people, and the cats would recognize me." Although a love for animals is a prerequisite for the humans who work with them, that love is not always reciprocated. "The animals generally aren't grateful when they wake up from being sedated. They might want to eat you," Wolff notes.

Her favorite story from among dozens is her "out-of-body experience" with a South American anteater called a tamandua. The animal was being held on its back by its keeper as the vet bent over to get a blood sample from the tail. In a flash, the tamandua's "extremely long, extremely sticky tongue went up my nose and tickled my brain. In spite of this experience, we'll have these animals in the park!"

Among the vet staff, most have favorite animals and specialties. Wolff likes birds, turtles, and primates; Mark Stetter works a lot with reptiles and amphibians.

Barb Mangold and Martha Weber are generalists, while Michele Miller likes hoofed animals and immunology.

A zoo vet's work is extremely physical. Tools of the trade include opera-length rubber gloves for delivering babies, extra-big thermometers, and anesthetics administered by blow darts and jab sticks. There's even mandatory dart practice—the vets shoot air rifles at hay bales and take shots with dart sticks to make sure their aim is true when an animal must be sedated to receive veterinary help.

The overall philosophy is "prevention," says Wolff. "We give yearly physicals—vaccines, blood work, checking for abnormalities against the database established by observation, the initial quarantine exams, and the questionnaires from their old homes. Individual animals will have excellent care." For large groups of animals in the savannah—for example, the 100-plus guinea fowl—the vets rely on the keepers to report abnormalities and medicate the birds' feed if there's a problem. An undetected communicable disease could spell disaster for a flock.

Detecting problems in any wild animal can be next to impossible. "They hide their illness well because they will get ostracized and/or eaten if they show any weakness in the wild," points out Wolff.

One of the vets' big concerns is Florida's mild climate. "No winter means more of a problem with fleas, mosquitoes, and worms, biting this's and that's," says Wolff. Using integrated pest management techniques in concert with The Land pavilion staff at

Epcot, the staff of Disney's Animal Kingdom Theme Park hopes to minimize pesticide use. When a natural predator isn't available, they'll rely on strategic application of chemicals at vulnerable parts of pests' life cycles.

"Wild animals make horrible patients," says Wolff. The safari vehicles will temporarily stop their circuit of the savannah if an animal is down. The team will hustle out in trucks and bring the sick animal in for observation. And if the vet staff needs outside help, they'll call in specialists from the University of Florida in Gainesville or, in the case of primates, human doctors.

Building Disney's Animal Kingdom Theme Park from the ground up presents the vets with "an extraordinary opportunity to maintain the animals in optimum health," Wolff proclaims. "With computerized records and our commitment to the animals, we deliver the best care we can."

Opposite: Grant's zebra; above: white rhinoceros; below: male African lion.

> *I think our back-of-house areas will impress the zoo community far more than our onstage spaces will. This brand-new facility has luxuries that few zoos enjoy.*
>
> RICK BARONGI,
> DIRECTOR OF
> ANIMAL PROGRAMS

Female sable antelope.

HOUSING BEHIND THE SCENES

The first introduction to Disney's Animal Kingdom Theme Park for every animal is their offstage housing. Just as a new house pet is kept in one room until it gets used to its surroundings, the animals spend weeks or months getting used to what some zoos call night houses; at Disney's Animal Kingdom they are called "back of house." These buildings are cutting-edge, built with care, consultation, and few compromises.

Three things are key to the design: safety for the animals, safety for the keepers, and a good connection to the onstage area—an easy passage for the animals as they travel out in the morning and back in at evening.

Animal care issues are paramount. Stalls are accessible, easily visible, easy to clean. Since animals coming from various institutions are introduced to one another in the houses, various devices facilitate the stages of getting acquainted. At first, the animals can see each other—or not, depending on the species. The next phase is to see and sniff one another. The last step is touch.

Maternity facilities have been designed so that mother and babies have a private stall; heated coils in the floor keep the area warm. The buildings are climate-controlled. Skylights and huge windows provide sunshine, and fresh air circulates through the buildings. "These are the lightest and airiest buildings ever built for animals," according to Barongi. "The light is just as much for the keepers. We've all had to work in dark, small, damp holding areas. They are depressing, for us and for the animals."

Disney's Animal Kingdom Theme Park represents a paradigm shift in the animal care community. In zoos, any money left over from a new exterior exhibit goes into a holding area that probably already exists and is being modified. During the design of Disney's Animal Kingdom park, the holding areas were budgeted for before the onstage habitats were designed. The on- and offstage costs were split about 50-50.

The keepers' offices are almost all on-line. Computer terminals will help keepers record the most minute observations, which will become part of the massive database on the animal collection.

Keeper safety is maintained through sturdy barriers and strong gates. There is thorough access to animals, from physical checks to observation decks to on- and offstage video cameras.

Quarantines, periods of observation and evaluation, were mandated for all animals. "No one has a quarantine building like we have," boasts Rick Barongi. Most places put animals temporarily in their vet facility or in an isolated paddock. "Here we have a quarantine building that can house a tiger and a gorilla and a dik-dik—all at once."

Procedures at Disney's Animal Kingdom Theme Park include keeping members of the same species together, comprehensive vet exams, and a "getting to know you" period for keepers. Some animals completed their quarantines in another part of Florida. Those who moved in first used their houses as quarantine sites. Young male gorillas were quarantined in the mandrill house while the family troop moved into the house they all now share. With quarantines successfully completed—no medical problems apparent and the animals used to each other and their quarters—it was time to introduce them to their expansive "onstage" habitats.

The giraffe barn includes a squeeze stall or "hugger" that has doors that open at strategic levels. It looks like the old joke wall on *Laugh-In*, but instead of Jo Anne Worley popping out you might see a spotted rump or a limpid, long-lashed eye.

Video cameras—controllable by guests at Conservation Station as well as keepers—have swivels and zooms that literally reveal flies on the walls, as well as animal behavior. The hippo houses feature covered outdoor swimming pools so the residents can cool off without burning their sun-sensitive skin.

The elephant barn is a marvel of engineering. "It's built like Jurassic Park," laughs Rick Barongi. Constructed to withstand the 10,000 pounds of vertical stress a bull elephant is capable of inflicting with his head, the cream and periwinkle–colored building has 16-foot-high bright purple and silver fencing made of 12-inch-square horizontal bars. Enormous gates roll on wheels. Inside the airy skylit barn, a forest of purple poles a foot in diameter cluster to make stalls. The poles are set far enough apart for people

to squeeze through, but elephants can't. Two stalls for bull elephants are separated from the double and single stalls. The keepers' office is on the second floor, with a balcony for viewing, to give the humans an overhead perspective on their charges. An outdoor hydraulic squeeze chute is designed for veterinary procedures and emergencies. Thick pistons compress metal bars along the elephant's sides, and 6-inch webbing straps support its belly as keepers and vets work on the animal.

For invertebrates, there are strict quarantine protocols because many insects are designated as "pest" species by agencies that grant permits. The collection of exotic bugs at Disney's Animal Kingdom Theme Park must remain in their environments to protect Florida's ecology. Detailed U.S. Department of Agriculture and state guidelines are observed every day. The insect rooms are controlled, with first and second entry ports. Super-fine mesh covers all the specially designed vents. Everything that comes out is frozen or sterilized by autoclave. For the staff, and for Florida's environment, adherence to these procedures is vital.

BEGINNING TO BUILD

At Walt Disney Imagineering, the elation at the formal media announcement quickly gave way to the adrenaline rush of staffing up to build Disney's Animal Kingdom™ Theme Park. New team members were joining the burgeoning group of ride experts, architects, estimators, artists—the many disciplines that comprise a fully fledged Imagineering design team.

A SHORT COURSE ON DISNEY'S ANIMAL KINGDOM

Newcomers to the team would attend an orientation meeting to get an overview of the park. Gathering in a room with scale models, slides, and renderings on the wall, new team members met the core group—Jack Blitch, the project manager; show producers Kelley Forde, Ann Malmlund, and Skip Lange; head writer Kevin Brown; design administrator Patsy Tillisch; animal operations director Rick Barongi; and chief designer Joe Rohde, who guided the neophytes through the basics of the park. Once the newcomers were acquainted with the project, it would be up to them to carry out the ideas developed during the last five years. Rohde would first explain the basic theme of the park—the human love for animals—and the background of its development. Then he conducted a tour of the park the new team members would have a hand in creating. The photographs in this chapter, accompanied by Rohde's comments, record the highlights of such a tour.

Construction workers swarmed over the site, creating the underpinnings of everything from rocks to trees to buildings from structural steel and concrete. More than 2,600 men and women labored on the park on the busiest days.

Oasis is a radical idea—an entry not through a traditional retail corridor like Main Street at Disneyland® Park, but a cool, green decompression zone, a rockwork idyll of waterfalls and landscaping that allows guests an immediate contact with exotic, beautiful animals, like colorful birds and sloths and tree kangaroos. It's a meandering path of discovery that keeps guests' views controlled and contained until they cross the bridge over Discovery River.

At the bridge, guests finally get their first look at the Tree of Life, the fantastic, towering icon of the park. Rising from a lush island, the 140-foot trunk is covered with animals that seem to emerge from the bark—a potent symbol of the interconnectedness of all living things.

Surrounding the Tree of Life are meadows for animals chosen for their beauty and playful behavior—otters and lemurs and cranes and storks. Inside is a 3-D film-and-effects extravaganza that celebrates Earth's most numerous and misunderstood life forms—insects—in a show called *It's Tough to Be a Bug*.

Around the Tree of Life is Safari
Village, where equatorial architecture meets Hawaiian shirts and
Mexican folk art. This is our
many-colored "Main Street," with
shops and dining. It also functions
as our hub; it's the place from
which our guests depart on every
adventure. An exuberant, innocent
love of animals has motivated the
use of folk art–inspired animal
forms on every available surface,
from walls and ceilings to win-
dowsills and gable ends.

Discovery River has two docks for the boats that ply the waters, gliding past the villages that are stepping-off points for safari adventures. Certain things can be seen only from the boats—like a fire-breathing dragon hidden in a cave—so this is an attraction as well as a transportation system.

Across the river is Harambe, a re-creation of a present-day village in eastern Africa that's on the edge of a large preserve. After passing through the main street, guests can board a safari vehicle at the huge old baobab for a look at animals. In Harambe we'll give guests a sense of Africa today. The safari's story is about the challenges Africans face, especially with regard to poaching and population pressures.

In the 100-acre African safari we have an upland forest, two savannahs, and lots of water. On opening day, we'll have well over 400 animals—from hippos and elephants to vultures and warthogs—and we can hold about twice that many.

Thirty-six guests per vehicle experience huge vistas that will look just like Africa. It will seem—and in many cases be true—that there are no barriers between animals and guests and between groups of different animals. A vehicle driver interacts with a ranger and a researcher who communicate with us by radio. The driver can point out interesting things along the way.

This is no ordinary safari. We have a story to tell, and we offer an adventure to be experienced. There are collapsing bridges and flooded-out places, and we skid and bump along. Then poachers are spotted in the park; they may have gotten hold of an elephant matriarch. We go off the beaten path on a dangerous mission to help the rangers find the poachers and the elephant.

After the safari, guests will be able to see small animals like meerkats and mole rats and birds on the Gorilla Falls Exploration Trail. Harambe has created this aviary and research complex to introduce its own population, as well as tourists, to wildlife and the work of field biologists. The climax of the trip is an immersion, by means of a bridge, into Gorilla Falls, where two troops of gorillas will be living on either side of the guests. It will seem as if there is nothing separating guests and gorillas but a grassy slope and a stand of bamboo.

DOTTED LINES INDICATE PLANTERS
IN ROCKWORK

FICUS IN PLANTER
ARTIFICIAL VINES BELOW

2 ROWS OF ARTIFICIAL BAMBOO (1 FOR G
- 1 FOR GUESTS) MIXED WITH REAL BAMB

UNDERGROUND GORILLA VIEWING
ENTRANCE

BAMBOO SPROUTS ABOVE IN
ROCKWORK PLANTER APPEAR TO
BE CONTINUATION OF ARTIFICIAL
BAMBOO BELOW

LAST BRIDGE FROM
GORILLA VALLEY

GRAPHICS LOCATION

BAMBOO GORILLA LOOK - IN

9 JUN '94
SHUMATE

N.T.S

SK · 55

Our other E-ticket attraction is Countdown to Extinction. To get there, guests will enter DinoLand, U.S.A., a tribute to our American love of dinosaurs, from tacky roadside attractions to serious scientific inquiry. The bridge from Safari Village is dominated by a huge Brontosaurus skeleton. DinoLand, U.S.A., is a hybrid: part wacky souvenir stand and part dinosaur dig. It is populated by professors and graduate students. Essentially, the students are pranksters, while the professors are voices of authority.

The Boneyard is for kids to play at being paleontologists. They can slide down debris chutes or bang on bone xylophones or dig for fossils, while studying the area for clues about how and why the dinosaurs lived and died.

Restaurantosaurus carries out the story of students and professors—it's their dorm and rec hall and cafeteria. Along Cretaceous Trail visitors will see animals and plants that have survived from prehistory.

And then there's the Countdown to Extinction attraction. So many early visitors to DinoLand, U.S.A., came up with questions that the Dino Institute was built to serve as a discovery center and ongoing research lab "dedicated to uncovering the mysteries of the past." Guests will wait in areas filled with museum-quality displays about dinos while learning that they can participate in a time-travel experiment to rescue a living dinosaur and return it to the present.

The eccentric and iconoclastic Dr. Grant Seeker takes the controls of the time-travel vehicle, and guests get a jolting, terrifying ride back to the moment a huge meteor struck Earth and destroyed the dinosaurs. Our dinosaurs, the biggest *Audio-Animatronics®* figures ever created, will be incredibly lifelike. This will be our big thrill ride.

Finally, the message portion of our park is most overtly expressed at Conservation Station. To get there from Harambe, you take the Wildlife Express, an incredibly beat-up old warhorse of a train. The train line runs along some of the back-of-house areas to let guests see the night housing for animals behind the scenes of the African safari.

Everything in this park can be traced back to a love for animals—Conservation Station especially. Because we love them, we've gone through all the other adventures to see and understand them. Now we want to do everything we can to protect them.

Conservation Station has the only direct animal contact in the whole park—the Affection Section. Inside the building are shows about the rain forest and marine environments, shows that feature animals and people we call Eco Heroes, as well as windows literally on the behind-the-scenes workings of the animal side of the park, from a veterinary operating room to a nursery. Everywhere will be the message that people are responsible for animals and that we can make a difference—that there is work to be done. We encourage people to get involved with organizations in their hometowns—zoos or conservation groups or whatever—because hopefully they have been inspired by their visit here. And hopefully you have been inspired too.

MEANWHILE, BACK IN FLORIDA

The 600 acres that were to become Disney's Animal Kingdom Theme Park didn't look like much in the summer of 1995. Bulldozers had lumbered over the site a year earlier to clear the agricultural land, saving most of the native oaks. The site was flat and high, mostly sandy, with the long west side sloping to the east.

On August 7, 1995, earth-moving vehicles began the process of building a theme park. First, there was destruction, seeming chaos, and lots of dirt. The fine, sandy grit flew through the air on windy days, bogged down huge vehicles on rainy days, and supported little vegetation.

Slowly, the asphalt ring road emerged around the park. The guest parking lot was paved first, to provide a home for the dozens of contractors from around the country who would be called to the site during the two years of construction.

The great canal running through the northern end of the site, designed years before by master planners for Walt Disney World® Resort, would not be able to handle the water that would pour off the site once the sculpting of the land began. Digging down just 30 to 45 centimeters brought groundwater to the surface. Detention ponds were created around the property to hold the runoff—as much as 10 million gallons of water pumped off each day—that would eventually be released to wetlands. Huge concrete drainage pipes, some 7 feet in diameter, were installed as deep as 28 feet underground, part of more than 60 miles of underground pipe.

Imagineering project managers Jack Blitch and Walter Wrobleski oversaw the early construction phases. Wrobleski, who coordinated the construction management of the park, was pleased with the early development of the site. The first package of blueprints contained detailed information of incredible definition. "It all made sense," according to Wrobleski, "the roads, the facilities, the underground layout. We could do the primary and secondary utilities at the same time, and that saved us a lot of time and money. It set the pace for success."

Meanwhile, back in Glendale, the work of the design team was far from over. Successive layers of finishes for buildings and shows, interiors and exteriors, were being created and committed to. As design deadlines were met, documents went out the door and into the field, or out to vendors for manufacture. The team, which had been operating as a skeleton crew, grew astronomically, quickly.

PHYSICAL PLANTS

One of the biggest investments and biggest conceptual leaps forward for the Animal Kingdom project was the landscaping. The vast catalogue called for more than 4 million plants, from huge trees to individual shoots of grass. The number of species of grasses exceeded 300. More than 770,000 shrubs and nearly 70,000 trees were planted in Africa alone.

The staff of eight landscape architects all had Disney theme park experience and had learned their craft at the feet of the legendary Bill Evans. Disneyland and Walt Disney World master landscaper and an acknowledged leader in the field, Evans pioneered landscape design for theme parks based on a three-part precept. The first consideration was guest comfort—shade and shelter. The second was screening visual intrusions—creating a berm, a ring of earth and vegetation surrounding the park, to hide the real world—or using strategic plantings that camouflaged a building or electronics or lighting. The third principle was

Imagineering landscape architect Bill Evans (left) pioneered plants as characters in Disneyland Park. Paul Comstock (right) continued his legacy and built an ecosystem at Disney's Animal Kingdom Theme Park.

Left: full-grown trees from around the world became part of the "instant landscape" at Disney's Animal Kingdom Theme Park. Above: Paul Comstock collects camellia seeds in the mountain wilds of Szechwan, China.

8 5

In Nepal, Paul Comstock had his most memorable experience: "I had botanized the Royal Chitwan preserve, in 1992, and had ridden on an elephant named Durgha Kali. I returned five years later, and this elephant kept sniffing me. The mahout [elephant handler] said the animal recognized me. I rode her every day and told the mahout what I was doing—collecting seeds in order to grow plants for an elephant habitat. He 'explained' this to Durgha Kali, and she actually harvested her favorite delicacies for me, using her trunk and passing the seeds over her back and into my hands."

telling a story through the landscape—creating the right look for the setting, from the mixed broadleaf forest of Tom Sawyer's Mississippi River banks to the serene gardens of Japan.

Together, the Animal Kingdom landscape group, led by Evans and Paul Comstock, came up with a rethink of the landscape's role in Disney's Animal Kingdom Theme Park. "Landscape *is* the set; it *is* the show," was Comstock's call to arms.

The team knew they needed large numbers of plants that were untried in Orlando's climate, which, though usually mild year-round, can have occasional nights of hard frost. They used the vast knowledge that had been built up over 40 years of nurturing Disney's lushly and lovingly planted resorts. Says Comstock, "Orchestrating the field installation with Mother Nature is a lot like playing music. It's improvisational landscape jazz that incorporates Darwinian design. We're creating an ecosystem and seeing what wins out in five years."

The landscape architects contacted suppliers all over America, arranging for plants to be propagated in temperate zones in California, Arizona, Maryland, and Florida, choreographing carefully timed production and shipments. Two growing seasons were called for so that the landscape would be well established when the animals came to call it their home. Using "accelerators" at the Disney tree farm, which is adjacent to the Animal Kingdom property, Imagineers coaxed saplings into good-size trees in just over a year's time.

The planners created a "heritage area" of growing trees on the berm, where they could go to replace plants that died. A browse farm—acacia, hibiscus, bamboo—would provide food for the leaf-eating animals. The planners carefully checked the lists with animal care experts to make sure vegetation in the animal habitats wasn't harmful or invasive.

Plant procurement was challenging, inspiring botanizing expeditions to distant lands, and leading Imagineers to develop relationships so they could tap knowledge and resources from experts around the globe.

In five years, Comstock visited Madagascar, South Africa, Kenya, Tanzania, Tasmania, Namibia, China, Thailand, Indonesia, and Singapore, collecting seeds and shoots and making contacts with nurseries and botanical gardens.

Acquiring full-size plants through the "nurseryman's grapevine" could lead to unexpected benefits for the plants' former owners. The team bought a huge stand of African date palms; the purchase price contributed to the construction of a badly needed children's daycare center. In another case, the purchase of a grove of "naturalized" giant timber bamboo paid for a new kitchen for a Georgia farmhouse. Ancient cycads, survivors of the Cretaceous Era that were slated for DinoLand, U.S.A., were found in Florida and from a collector in Eagle Rock, California.

Comstock traveled the world gathering flowering trees, other broadleaf trees, succulents, vines, and grasses. Some were collected for a specific use—the African thorned acacia and baobab trees "say Africa," according to Comstock. "We needed African species to give a golden savannah tone." For the fabulous flowering landscapes of the Oasis and Safari Village, the team relied on the usually congenial climate of Orlando, "greenhouse summer and cool winters," to amass a collection from every tropical, sub-tropical, and temperate zone on Earth, and from every continent except Antarctica.

"DESIGN FOR THIS!"

Imagineering's engineers were getting a short course in load management for elephants. They were immersed in designing back-of-house buildings made of tubes, not angles, so that birds or rats couldn't nest in them. Before structural engineer Leland Rorex bestowed on a drawing his seal of approval (literally—he uses an embossed seal when he signs off on each blueprint), he checked for details that experienced zoo designers had specified. "We couldn't use bolts anywhere near elephants or gorillas or monkeys; they are too dextrous. We had to design for the fact that a lion can leap—with an antelope in its mouth—ten feet high."

Rorex was one of the first California-based Imagineers on the site, which was, by spring 1996, the focus of a huge sculpt-ing effort. Lakes and hills were being created, and the first of 150 free-standing buildings were beginning to appear. The construction strategy, once the infra-structure was in place, was to begin in the south and north areas of the park—the Oasis and the African savannah—and work toward the center—DinoLand, U.S.A., Safari Village, and Harambe. The Tree of Life was begun, its massive conical under-pinnings in place, as soon as Discovery River was scooped out.

Some 4½ million cubic yards of dirt were moved; 2 million came from off-site. Enormous vehicles barreled up ramps, hauling huge loads of dirt from the riverbed while pumps kept it temporarily dry. Discovery River—only 8 feet deep—is designed to be a natural part of the water systems in the area, so the bottom was not

The Tree of Life was given extra scrutiny as "the single most challenging structure on the property," according to Imagineer Leland Rorex. An engineering professor oversaw the project. The bottom half of the trunk is designed using off-shore oil-drilling technology and 36-inch-diameter pipe. A wind tunnel study was commissioned for the tree branches; the leaves streamline into the wind and can withstand a blow of nearly 100 mph. Right: the hexagonal structure for the in-tree theater ceiling.

paved. The riverbanks have been engineered to be normally 18 inches below high water level so the system can ebb and flow.

Though off to a great start, within six months of beginning construction the team was under the gun, "behind by three or four weeks out of a year and a half schedule," according to project VP Wrobleski. "It could have been disastrous for us, but the contractors persevered and got back on schedule. They really poured on the manpower." With, of course, the assistance of the Imagineering team. "For every four contractors, there are eight of us," he explains. "We share the risk, because schedule means so much to us all along the line."

Close supervision has been necessary from the beginning so that there are a minimum of fire hydrants in sloth exhibits or few drainage grates where carpeted walkways would eventually go. As estimator Jerre Kirk says, "We have to put the ears on it"—give it Disney quality and attention to detail from the very beginning.

A classic "putting the ears on it" discipline for Imagineering is making concrete "look like anything except concrete," says landscape planner John Shields. Concrete is used to make rocks, riverbanks, trees, and termite mounds. It is sculpted to create dino bones and weathered plaster buildings, fences and waterfalls. It's even used to make dirt—in the most spectacular example, the cracked, pitted, washboarded, flooded, almost-overgrown "dirt road" for the Africa vehicles.

Left: Imagineering landscape planner John Shields created special stamps to mimic the hooves of antelopes in the "muddy" road. The crew threw twigs and gravel on the road and matched its color to the surrounding dirt. "We ruined a lot of concrete finishers," Shields laughs. Used to making smooth sidewalks, the contractors were asked to actually create potholes. "One guy really got into it," says Shields. "He decorated the brim of his hard hat with gravel and glued a model truck on it." Shields literally threw himself into his work, wrapping himself in a plastic sheet and rolling in wet concrete to create an "elephant wallow." Opposite: because the dirt road in the African safari needed to remain the way it was designed—with bumps and grinds coming at carefully orchestrated places along a ride track that would be used daily by fully loaded trucks—Imagineers created a reinforced concrete pathway 7½ inches deep. It had the ruts and potholes in place, and even carefully located planters so grass would grow between the "wheel tracks" of the safari vehicles.

CONSTRUCTION COORDINATION

Coordination among the contractors and the Imagineers was vital. One group lagging behind would mean other milestones falling like dominoes—and the potential derailment of the whole project. Missing any one of the critical dates for completion of four crucial elements—underground utilities, building foundations, the Countdown to Extinction, and the Tree of Life—would put the entire project in jeopardy.

To ensure that all contractors and managers communicated effectively, Animal Kingdom management instituted a mandatory morning meeting on the site. Every day the general contractors' representatives met in the main trailer for an hour. A contractor who needed to plant a 20-ton tree in a courtyard—a tree around which the building would have to be constructed—could borrow the crane scheduled to set the building's steel frame. The representatives could work out logistics in advance and prevent conflicts in the field, where every minute counted over the course of the two-and-a-half-year construction schedule.

This page, top: head of
Saltasaurus; middle left:
Imagineers sculpt the full-size
Parasaurolophus; middle right:
baby Parasaurolophuses cuddle;
below: an Alioramus swallows a
meal on the run.
Opposite left: Imagineer Jack
Raupach reaches into the
Alioramus; right: Gene Wiskerson
creates a model of Styracosaurus.

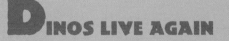

DINOS LIVE AGAIN

Creating believable dinosaurs in Countdown to Extinction was a high priority, handed down from CEO Michael Eisner. The biggest *Audio-Animatronics®* figures ever produced, the T. Rex–size dinosaurs represented a huge outlay of money and hours.

Goddard or Jeff Kilbane. Animal Kingdom design chief Joe Rohde, a passionate amateur dinophile, kibitzed on hip joint placement and helped with coloration. Casey Brennan, a geologist-turned-artist in charge of the Boneyard, offered suggestions.

The Imagineers came up with a new method of creating *Audio-Animatronics®* figures for Countdown to Extinction. The first step was to mock up the movement on computers. A small model raptor would then be built to test the hypotheses. It incorporated powerful new chips to control a myriad of subtle movements, new types of machinery to create the motion, and a new underlying armature. Imagineers also had to create innovative ways to join the heavy skin (up to 500 pounds) to the moving metal parts. At the first formal review, when the dinosaurs were fully assembled, moving majestically and lit dramatically in the warehouse, a visibly moved Eisner said it best: "It's the first time I've been sorry they are extinct."

The Imagineering team designing the creatures consulted paleontologists and pored over books to make sure the shapes and sizes, movements, skin texture, and coloration would be authentic and dramatic. Miniature models of the dinosaurs in the show were scaled up to full-size clay sculptures. The towering heads of the Iguanodon and Saltasaurus almost scraped the cavernous ceiling of the Tujunga, California, warehouse. Show designer Paul Torrigino would scramble up on an 18-foot ladder to talk about the jaw fold or teeth with sculptors Scott

SHAPING THE KINGDOM

The "back stories" for each land or area created by the core team during the development of Disney's Animal Kingdom™ Theme Park became the jumping-off point for a variety of disciplines. Collaborating and elaborating on the basic ideas, designers called on tricks of many trades to help support the stories. Their contributions, conceived at drawing tables and implemented throughout the Animal Kingdom park, may be subtle, sometimes nearly visceral, but in aggregate they create the convincing environment, the completely immersive experience, that Disney theme parks are known for around the world.

THE WONDERFUL WORLD OF COLOR

Senior show designer Katie Olson starts working on detailed "color boards" as soon as the architectural drawings are complete. Conferring with show designers and architects about the history, mood, and function of the park buildings, she creates renderings that begin to tell the story.

Working directly on architectural elevations with hand-mixed acrylic paint and colored pencil, Olson creates meticulous works of art that become references for plaster, graphics, prop, and lighting designers. Her exquisite miniatures are cross-referenced to paint colors, and become official contract documents. "By the end of a project, I've done scores of boards, many more than once," Olson says. "I end up memorizing colors. I'll go out to the park and say, 'Shouldn't that be number 8663 on that eave?'"

Inspired by the team's first trip to Africa, the dramatic thatched baobab in the village of Harambe required close collaboration among many Imagineering disciplines, including design and sculpture, structural engineering, and construction coordination.

Olson evaluates the palette of the park and groups of buildings, looking for a "sweep of color." Warm colors are friendly—they draw the eye in. Adding color value brings buildings up to the foreground. Color is most intense up close to the guests, focusing attention and importance on architectural elements.

Painters use color to fix and conceal mistakes. If a roofline is showing, they can find a color to match the surrounding foliage and camouflage it. In the field, Olson travels around the park, looking for electrical boxes in planters and painstakingly matching the box color to the plants that surround it.

With 25 years of experience to guide them, the Disney painters know that in Florida, the bright sunshine intensifies colors, so they add gray to each hue. Pure white can sometimes turn blindingly blue and a pale color can seem white.

The riot of color in Safari Village was a challenge to keep in balance. "It doesn't have to be recognizable as anywhere in particular, and that gives you a lot of freedom," Olson says. "But you have to respect the form of the architecture. We used a lot of Caribbean color and references like Mexican wedding dresses and Oaxacan carved animals." A classically trained artist, Olson sees her job as a bold blend of theater design and art. She learned what she knows from Walt Disney Imagineering senior vice president John Hench. "He's the guru of color. He taught me so much about how very vital color is to our theme parks. If the color design successfully supports the overall story we are telling, the environment becomes that much more magical for our guests."

MOVE OVER, MARTHA

While Olson was creating the exterior look of the buildings, the interior designers were concocting unusual treatments and fixtures for shops and restaurants. Like all Imagineers, they started with the story.

In DinoLand, U.S.A., where the wacky roadside souvenir stand known as Chester and Hester's Dinosaur Treasures was formerly a gas station, a leaning stack of oil cans has become a unique hat rack. The museum-like rotunda within the Dino Institute strikes a more formal tone, with marble floors and glass cases for dioramas and displays of fossils.

Restaurantosaurus, now the living quarters of the dig team, was the original, funky Dino Institute. The great room is the old exhibit hall, with layers of old and new dino displays and the accumulated historical ephemera of the dig site. The dining space was broken into rooms with different functions that help tell the stories of generations of grad students and professors. For the bunk room, designers created a tent-like ceiling made from two layers of canvas with a layer of glass in the middle. The team even purchased an old Airstream trailer from Imagineer Todd Beeson's grandmother to tack onto the side of the building. With cozily upholstered red vinyl booths, it's a rec room extraordinaire.

Above: at Asia Bridge, a painter replicates the ruddy colors of Nepalese brickwork.
Below: a miniature masterpiece, a color board for **Tusker House Restaurant** *in Harambe.*

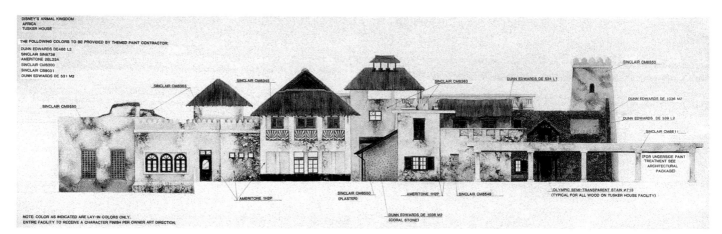

Chester and Hester's Dinosaur Treasures is the ultimate affectionate tribute to roadside Americana. A former gas station, the place (so the story goes) was owned by amateur dinosaur aficionados Chester and Hester. Just outside the bounds of the Dinosaur Institute's property, the shop bristles with tacky, spangly signs and is crammed with merchandise of sometimes questionable educational value. The Institute wants to buy and raze the place, but Chester and Hester's unidentified heirs have as good a sense of humor as the originators. They won't sell. Tiny plastic dinosaurs ride rickety, dinosaur-themed trains suspended from the "grimy" ceiling while others flee fake lava flows in the highest corners. Years of thumbtacks and scribbles "scar" the walls near the phones. Everything that can be turned into a dinosaur has been, including old oil cans, rulers, and flexible pipe.

66We break the rules. It's architecture that entertains.99

DAVID BRICKEY,
INTERIOR DESIGNER

DOTTING I-BEAMS AND CROSSING T-SQUARES

Like their colleagues in set design, architecture, and lighting, members of the interiors staff are highly cognizant of where heating and air-conditioning ducts are placed. They worry about light and sprinkler locations, and accessibility regulated by the Americans with Disability Act. They inspect materials as they are installed, working to ensure that "Disney details" are not overlooked. Because their creations are so touchable, they also worry about safety, "little fingers getting caught or heads banging into shelves," says interior designer David Brickey.

They also have to keep in mind the uses of their buildings, as they interface with colleagues who work with foods and merchandise at Walt Disney World® Resort. They help with kitchen design. They design break rooms for cast members. They worry about how guests will circulate and where to locate cash registers, or POS's (point of sale). Their conversation is sprinkled with a glossary of terms for things that hold merchandise: bunkers, gondolas, spinners, and universal posts. The interiors budget covers carpets and antifatigue mats, restaurant tables and chairs. Staff members buy the trashcans and benches; for Disney's Animal Kingdom Theme Park, many are made of recycled materials.

Inspiration for interiors comes from the story, from trips to foreign countries, and from a library of samples, acquired from vendors all over the world, housed at the Imagineering offices. The designers visit trade shows, leaf through catalogues, and surf the Internet looking for unusual finishes, colors, and custom-created tiles or carpets. Ninety percent of the interior finishes at Disney's Animal Kingdom park are custom-created. Very few walls sport paint brushed on straight from the can. Most have been specially sponged, ragrolled, glazed, drybrushed, or cellophaned.

The buildings in Safari Village are individually themed around a unique, over-the-top salute to animals. Island Mercantile, the biggest shop, features animals that migrate and work—whales and wildebeests, ants and bees. Geese morphing into airplanes and pulleys shaped like beavers hang from the ceiling. In Disney Outfitters, an upscale clothing store, elegant animals of the six directions—north, south, east, west, above, and below—decorate the space. In Beastly Bazaar, animals from fresh and salt water cavort on walls, ceiling, and floor. Creature Comforts, the children's store, features animals with stripes and spots. The sly theme of the *Flame Tree Barbecue* is predator and prey—prey are painted on the tables, predators are cast into the chairs.

The designers went to Asia to work with Balinese sculptors and to Mexico to find basket weavers who could fashion wicker kangaroos to hold merchandise.

"We want to intrigue people," designer Brickey says of creating Safari Village's incredible interiors. He loves the playfulness of the end result, achieved through years and years of attention to details like custom-textured concrete floors, pebble and broken tile mosaics, and intricately patterned wood grilles. "We want guests to walk through and see everything, for the pure delight of it. I just do it for fun!"

Four hours up a dirt-and-boulder mountain road in Oaxaca, Mexico, Imagineering's interiors team found Rojelio Blas and his family. Rojelio carves fantastically shaped animals, then his wife and kids paint them in bright colors and whimsical patterns. The Imagineers ordered 300 bats, 120 bugs, and 150 butterflies to hang in **Pizzafari.**

This page and overleaf: for Pizzafari's five dining rooms, 34 stunning murals were painted by Imagineering veteran Frank Armitage and his artist daughter Nicole. Oversized animals rendered in bright colors look down from the walls of one room, while animals that hide in their environments peep out in another. Creatures that carry their houses on their backs—turtles and snails and hermit crabs—creep along in a third room. Another theme is animals that come out at night. There is even a whole room based on animals that hang upside down.

MAJOR PROPS TO THIS TEAM

Prop designers work on both the interior and exterior of buildings. They dress out the safari vehicles and Wildlife Express carriages with authentically bruised luggage and dinged-up equipment. Even the huge Brachiosaur skeleton at the entrance to DinoLand, U.S.A., is considered a prop.

Props provide the finishing, authentic touches that imply that the real inhabitants will be right back. "I'm a storyteller," explains prop designer Ken Gomes. "I don't just stuff a space."

For Harambe, Gomes bought taxi-loads of canned goods, cots, and camping paraphernalia from East African stores, arranged it in the lobby of his hotel, and photographed the lot. The puzzled staff guessed he was buying supplies for refugees. They remarked that groceries must be cheaper in Africa than in America. Gomes asked them to store his finds, but they told him to take the food to his room for safekeeping. On a final trip to town, he bought a couple of propane stoves. As he carried them upstairs, the clerks called, "We're sorry, sir! You can't cook in your room!"

Prop designers do a lot of shopping and bargaining. For vintage stuff, it's antiques stores and swap meets. To locate modern items, they usually go to the source. What they can't buy they have fabricated by the Imagineers at Walt Disney Imagineering's Tujunga, California, facility, or by outside vendors who specialize in things like Brachiosaur skeletons.

The huge skeleton on display in DinoLand, U.S.A., was fabricated from a cast of bones found by the staff of the Royal Tyrrell Museum of Paleontology. Located in Drumheller, Alberta, Canada, the museum is one of the fore-most fossil-studying institutions in North America.

While at the museum, prop buyers Michelle Rodriguez and Beverley Barritt were in ecstasy over the cast-off equipment that had been used on digs the previous summer. They bought it all—resin-imbedded aprons and already-rusted shovels—saving the project time and money. The museum staff were elated to add to their budget for new equipment. What Barritt couldn't find at the museum, she bought in Santa Monica ("I'm always the only woman in an old-tool shop") or at Home Depot. "I bury it for a bit in my garden, and it comes out just right," she laughs. Or she really saves the project money: "I get something for every park out of a trash can."

Above: Beverley Barritt adds finishing touches to a cabinet at Gorilla Falls Exploration Trail.
Below: the original concept sketch. Imagineering prop designers purchase or fabricate all the accoutrements, then install them in the proper location.

IT TAKES A VILLAGE . . .

To come up with the thousands of animal motifs used in Safari Village, Imagineering production designer Jenna Frere Goodman and colleague Ruben Viramontes first searched for images appropriate to each building's theme. Then they interpreted hundreds of animals in a naive folk style that reflected the design direction for each building: over-the-top Thai for *Flame Tree Barbecue*'s predators and prey; subdued, sophisticated colors for the animals of the six directions in Disney Outfitters; 1940s fruit-crate art as the inspiration for Island Mercantile's camels, wildebeests, ducks, and monarch butterflies—all creatures that work and migrate.

The animals appear on murals and as three-dimensional adornments for the buildings. It was decided that the approximately 1,500 carved wooden animals—props and interior and exterior architectural details—would be carved and painted in Bali. The artistic island in Indonesia was the perfect place to produce the carvings, both fanciful and faithful—the list includes "large goofy snails" and "mean green sea monsters," lemurs and leopards.

The images were carved with the help of full-scale paper templates fashioned by Goodman and Viramontes. Goodman journeyed to the island to paint with the Balinese for a week, producing the "first articles," which later would be copied in quantities. She was charmed by the experience with her fellow-artists: a gamelan orchestra accompanied them as they worked, and they sang when they painted. "It was magic," she says.

It was up to prop designer Ken Gomes to oversee the production of more than 100 hand-carved and -painted articles shipped each month to Florida; he moved to Bali and became a part of village life, attending weddings and funerals, acquiring "a sarong collection the envy of any Balinese," and giving Macarena lessons. Known as Wayan ("second-born") Sin Ken Ken ("no problem"), the imperturbable Imagineer went with the flow of Balinese life. One day a carver's kitchen collapsed, and everyone left work to rebuild it. Gomes' reaction was simply, "The sense of community here is refreshing." By following the rules—respecting the culture—he was able to run the best production house on the island. Besides, "the talent and skill you find in Bali is an incredible resource, like Europe a hundred years ago. They don't realize how gifted they are."

Above: at a Balinese carving studio, show producer Skip Lange inspects a sculpted sea horse destined for Safari Village. Such carved and painted motifs convey an exuberant love for animals in every form.
Overlay above: a rafter in Beastly Bazaar.
Overlay below: a monkey outside Disney Outfitters.

Achieving the right blend of vernacular equatorial architecture, which serves as the low-rise backdrop for the burgeoning animal motifs of Safari Village, took years of design trial and error. The Flame Tree Barbecue complex is Balinese in character, but an international assemblage of Imagineering architects—natives of Spain, Iran, the United States, and the Philippines—incorporated elements drawn from as far away as the American Southwest. Motifs, clockwise from top right: owl at **Flame Tree Barbecue**, snake and prey at **Flame Tree Barbecue**, snail on shutter at **Pizzafari**.

AGED TO PERFECTION

The Animal Kingdom park has an extremely "lived in" look that underlines the overall theme of nature's transcendence over human effort. Taking brand-new construction and giving it a vintage look blends art and science in the service of telling a story.

Executive production designer Ron Esposito directed a total crew of 200 painters and agers from Walt Disney World's painting powerhouses Buena Vista Construction Company and Central Shops. They fanned out around the Animal Kingdom park, basing their treatments on samples Esposito created by consulting with the show producers in each area. The painters came up with the final looks on walkways, rockwork, and buildings—everything from the slightly aged Countdown to Extinction building (only 10 years old) to the 40 or 50 years of the multi-use garage-turned-souvenir shop called Chester and Hester's Dinosaur Treasures.

"I was brought up in the movie business," explains Esposito. "The best production designers would paint a word picture about the set you had to create. It's the same way here. The most important part is the story line.

"Our buildings are the establishing shot," he explains in movie lingo. "They set the stage and tell the guest whether the attraction is cheerful or ominous, lighthearted or serious."

When Esposito and the show producer determine the story of a building, the next step is reference. On a five-day trip to Africa, Esposito shot 60 rolls of film of peeling doors and mossy buildings and signs. He also took chips off buildings, storing them in the empty film cans. He doesn't recommend this technique for would-be painters and agers: for his trouble, he had to endure a search by German customs agents in the Frankfurt airport. "They took me and my film cans to a lab. Twenty people used X-rays and microscopes on them, then they said, 'It's dirt.' Just like I tried to tell them!"

Reference is good—but it's not everything. "If you try to duplicate everything in nature it might be perceived as dirty," Esposito explains. "We give it the Disney twist—we use the psychology of color." They "sweeten" by adding chroma, enhancing the look, making it warm, "friendly-ing it up." "It's the feeling of color that draws people," Esposito says, "and how much color is used."

Color also includes painted effects—the use of washes to create shadows, forcing architecture that's only 2 inches deep to look more like 6 inches of relief. Highlights bring edges forward. Copper is toned down to a weathered green. Releasing agents added to paint make it crack, peel, and weather, giving it years of wear in a mere day or two.

All this has to be completely documented and replicable so that the look can be maintained. High-guest-use areas are typically "rehabbed" each night so they stay at the perfect pitch of old or new, pristine or beat up. That's in addition to a regular five-year rotation of paint maintenance for the whole park.

NEW BOATS FOR OLD

The need for aging extends to the safari vehicles and Discovery River boats. Inside the tents where vehicles are painted is a smell familiar to those who made models as kids. Painter Brian Wagner admits he was a model fanatic in his youth. Now he revels in creating "bug splats, textured mud, and bird doo," as well as rust and dents. "I think about how the mud goes on: what kinds of things the vehicle has run into over the years." His eyes take on a dreamy look. "I think I need some zebra hair over here."

Jack Plettinck led the crew that took the Discovery River boats, all nice and shiny from the boat manufacturer in Seattle, and roughed them up to fit the style of Disney's Animal Kingdom Theme Park. *The Darting Dragonfly, Otter Nonsense, Leaping Lizard, Crocodile Belle,* and *Hasty Hippo* were a mess when Plettinck was done with them. A boat owner since his teens, Plettinck applied his acrylic dings and dents with full cognizance of the hundreds of hazards—moorings, docks, submerged logs, and angry animals—the water craft would have encountered. "They are made out of metal, and they may get some new dents in the park," says Plettinck. "But the rust is all put on by us."

YEAH, WRITE

Once the sets are completed by painters and plasterers, props and lighting personnel, the work of writer Kevin Brown and his team fills in the theme park's stories with even more detail. Their words, from scripts to signage to file labels and posters, help the land the team created come alive.

Gorilla Falls Exploration Trail represents a "huge amount of mental—and finger—time," says Brown. Here guests are peeking over the shoulders of field workers at a research camp and conservation school. The characters in the cast have stories that need to come across on paper—on letters, field notes, sketches, bulletin boards, address labels—all specially created at Walt Disney Imagineering.

The first step for an immense project like this is inspiration. For Gorilla Falls, the genesis was a trip to the Kenyan highlands, where Brown made a visit to a ranch run by a former big-game hunter and his son. They had set up a school and a huge library focused on native wildlife and how to use it wisely and preserve it. A subsequent visit to Cynthia Moss's elephant research station in Amboseli National Park provided clues to how researchers live in the field. "They may not have much, but they all have a bulletin board full of photos of home, postcards, memos, and memorabilia," notes Brown.

The fictional cast of researchers each needed an individual identity. The only permanent member of the staff is the head of the project, Dr. K. Kulunda; the rest are visiting students from Africa, Europe, and America. The erudite Dr. Kulunda, who wonders why

one of the students has named her female hyena research subjects after first-century Roman women, is modeled on a junior high teacher whom Brown remembers well, a rotund little bald-headed man who loved his subject. Brown used the name of his second cousin for a researcher. And his telephone extension number at Imagineering appears on the P.O. box at Gorilla Falls.

Posters on the walls of Harambe were inspired by similar broadsides writer Kevin Brown saw in Africa. Graphic designers used examples Brown brought back to the United States to give his words the right look on the finished products. The Imagineering creations blend seamlessly with authentic tin signs purchased in Africa by prop buyers.

On his many trips to Africa, Kevin Brown collected printed ephemera—stickers, signs, pamphlets, and newspapers—for use by Imagineering graphic designers. His research in East Africa helped him cast his prose in Kenyan English, with "tweaked, third-world Victorian" phrasing like "Guests here will receive the highest facilitation." "It was a little dangerous," confides Brown. "The syntax can be intoxicating." With the help of a dictionary, Brown put any Swahili into roughly equivalent English, which was then vetted by a translator, Sara Mirza, who teaches at a Los Angeles university.

Brown mined the *Nairobi Times* obituaries for appropriate names. *The Daily Nation* inspired business ads like "The East African Seed Company—Always Sound and Reliable." A Kenyan book of folk tales provided a longer version of "When Hippo Was Hairy," the story of how hippos came to be naked, pink, short-tailed, and aquatic.

"It's a bit of a game," admits Brown. "We're creating notes, journals, jokes, thoughts, letters, and multiple addresses for people—and things—that have been around the world, from the field to zoos to universities. As with Tolkien, 'it grew in the telling.' As we developed Gorilla Falls we needed some graphics to fill in the story."

The many pages of writing created over several months "have an obsessive quality," says Brown. "Everything has to hang together. You can't make some of it up; it's a real subject. Our purpose is to give real information in a story context, and hopefully make people smile in the process."

THE ART OF RE-CREATING REALITY

In a Disney theme park, story is paramount, and sometimes the story is not fantasy but reality. At Disney's Animal Kingdom Theme Park, Africa is today, now—the village and safari must convince guests they are there. Imagineers are master "illusioneers" who create authentic-looking, authentic-feeling, authentic-sounding spaces. New ideas combine with tricks of various trades honed over 40-plus years in the business to form the physical basis for a willing suspension of disbelief— in other words, a surrender to the environment of the park.

INTO AFRICA, IN FLORIDA

The park's African savannah is a sweeping canvas of trees and waving grasses and rockwork, all of which is deliberately designed. While the hoofed animals roam in fields of 15 and 25 acres or more, most of the other animals are confined by cleverly placed barriers that you would find in any zoo. In zoos, you see the barriers, but at Disney's Animal Kingdom Theme Park, you don't.

In zoos, most barriers are water moats or dry double moats made of concrete and, if they are themed at all, just painted a neutral color. At Disney's Animal Kingdom Theme Park, things that keep animals within their exhibits are disguised. What would be a chain-link back fence at a zoo becomes here a steep slope smothered with plants. The classic sheer-sided, deep, and often dry concrete moats are there, but the edges are not fabricated in a straight line. They are disguised with plantings, broken up with rockwork, and stepped back from guests' sight lines. Fences are hidden behind geologic features.

Above: the rockwork arch of the klipspringer kopje (foreground) conceals the animals' night quarters, hidden inside the rugged habitat.
Below: a hawk's-eye-view of the warthog habitat reveals a typical moat structure on the savannah: steep-sided concrete ditches artfully concealed by natural landscape features.

Ironically, reports show producer Kelley Forde, "In Africa they hang hot-wires to discourage relocated elephants to keep off parts of the range. You'll never see that in our Africa."

Each time the design called for a barrier, the designers created a coherent story for it; they worked out how the river flowed, creating islands and riverbanks and logjams. Working the geological story into the landscape helps guests pick up the environmental integrity and accept that the settings are authentic.

The park's other ploy is to keep animals within the view of the guests. Onstage habitats are often long and narrow, strung along the winding vehicle ride track. Inviting shade trees, concrete feeders, and drinkers disguised as tree stumps or termite mounds encourage animals to assemble in picturesque groups.

Dead, weatherbeaten trees and branches placed around the habitats do everything from protecting shade plants to providing "cover" for concrete feeders. The trees also act as "exhibit furniture"—animals leave their scent marks on them or use them as scratching posts.

Another principle is to design the habitats on large, elevated areas. This keeps the animals at the eye level of guests, who are seated high in the safari vehicle. There's no feeling of human superiority; unlike in some zoos, guests won't look down on the animals. In fact, the psychology of some species—gorillas and big cats—indicates that they like to be superior to humans, and the designers have obliged.

During the safari, the vehicle bypasses service roads disguised onstage as faint, disused tracks. "This kind of attention to detail is a real luxury," says African safari architect Pat Janikowski, who has designed zoos around the world. "It sets Disney's Animal Kingdom apart."

Just as in Africa, where herders try to keep cows from mixing with big game, the Harambe reserve has cattle guards. These barriers discourage the Ukungu Forest herds from mixing with their counterparts on the west savannah. The guards act more as a visual barrier, rather than a physical one. "Most antelopes can jump them," explains landscape architect Duane Dietz. "The real, 'soft' barrier is the safari vehicle passing through, every half a minute, all day long."

The black rhino habitat is "fairly zoo-like," according to Janikowski. The rhinos should appreciate the mud wallows and the 8-foot-deep concrete pond. Hidden underwater and painted to match it, barriers keep rhinos on their side of the river.

The safari vehicle seems to plunge through Hippo River with the two-ton critters threatening to swamp the jeep from both sides. Actually, concrete fins with a 45-degree angle—called hippo bumpers—turn the beasts back from their pools' walls on both sides of the road. The angle is so steep that the animals can't get their feet up on them; the length of the fins also keeps the hippos in the center of the rivers so that the guests can see them. Water pumped over the ride path creates the illusion that the two pools are connected and that the vehicle is fording the river.

The west savannah, marked by large expanses of grasses that produce an almost painterly palette, is dotted with concrete termite mounds, some disguising feeders and drinking troughs, some just for show. The tall mounds with big columns are the ones ostensibly filled with "living" termites; the columns are chimneys used to vent hot air from the insects' metabolism. Older mounds have collapsed; observant guests will see deep parallel marks created by the claws of hungry aardvarks.

Modeled on a Masai corral, a boma is a cement block circle disguised by stripped tree trunks. It provides a structure keepers can use in order to pass between paddocks unobserved by guests. It also functions as a field hospital for injured animals that need vet assistance. On the vast expanse of the savannahs, keepers can visually check animals, again unobserved by guests, from ridges and hidden fence lines. Three video

animal cams—in the bank above the hippos, on the highest point of the savannah in a baobab tree, and hidden in the brushes of the mandrill exhibit—also help keepers survey the scene. Guests can control these cameras from Conservation Station.

The state-of-the-art elephant habitat, six acres devoted to the elephant family, is bisected by the vehicle track so that guests seated on both sides of the vehicle have a good view. The elephants have access to both sides of the habitat via a bridge that crosses over the ride track. The elephant causeway is themed as a long-abandoned railroad bridge. Native herons and egrets mix with the colony of African flamingoes on the island, which is shaped in three simple lobes (one of the park's traditional "hidden Mickeys," incorporated into the design by mischievous Imagineers). The elephants lumber into their pools on concrete stairs, which have dark treads and risers that match the water color. A steep turnback in the pool keeps the elephants from fording the water. The space, the lush vegetation, and the birds combine to form a convincing vision of Africa.

Opposite: before it was filled, the hippo habitat revealed the sheer banks that keep the animals in the river. Visible near the ride path are the "fins" that encourage the animals to stay in the middle of the water so guests can see them. Below, top: well out of sight of guests, a perimeter "ha-ha" fence runs at the edge of the berm, rising to the right. Heavy vegetation in front of the fence hides it and keeps hoofed animals from getting the running start needed to leap the 8-foot-high fence and its 3-foot turnback. Below, bottom: on a dry run, the safari vehicle passes the concrete bollards in the black rhino habitat. Hidden underwater, the uprights will keep the rhinos well back from the ride path.

SIGN UP NOW!

Imagineering's graphics department takes care of signage and other printed matter—more than 3,200 pieces in Disney's Animal Kingdom park. Signs must be legible and informative, but their theming is critical to the environmental style of storytelling. Signage both complements and completes an area. Large signs set the stage, with looks that range from whimsical to imposing. Small pieces provide details.

Early in the design process, good-looking logos and posters help "sell" a concept. The graphics folks were sworn to secrecy when they helped produce the colorful artwork that announced Disney's Animal Kingdom Theme Park to the media.

Because much of their work consists of large, permanent marquees, Imagineering graphic designers also have to think like engineers. They need to be sure that their three-dimensional creations stay put in 100-mph hurricane winds. Most signs are designed of durable, tested materials that will last for at least 10 years in Florida's heat, humidity, and fierce ultraviolet light.

The "touchability" of a graphic element is just as important—if it's within a guest's reach, it must be nearly indestructible. "If it looks like a piece of paper, chances are it's not," confides one designer. Often sign components—like the Tibetan-style prayer flags on the Caravan Stage marquee—are produced in multiples. They will be replaced every two to three years, meanwhile aging gracefully and mellowing into the landscape.

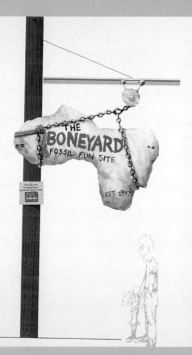

Using a Stegosaurus shoulder bone as the basis for the Boneyard marquee, graphic designers subtly modified it to take on the shape of Disney's Animal Kingdom before the Asia expansion. Note the "N" with arrow that points north, giving away the gag.

Departing Passengers Are Advised To Obtain Their Seats At Least Fifteen Minutes Prior To Listed Departure Time As The Train Will Depart Promptly On Schedule.

Advanced Booking for Upper Class Accommodation On Passenger Trains Will Only Be Accepted Without Payment Or Vouchers Subject To Payment Being Made 4 Weeks Before Scheduled Date Of Travel.

NEXT DEPARTING TRAIN

WILDLIFE EXPRESS To Conservation Station

Harambe boasts specially created signs inspired by printed matter collected on trips to East Africa, and include such details as the telephone authority logo (left) and the town's coat of arms (right). Above: the signs at the Harambe train station are authentically archaic in type style and wording.

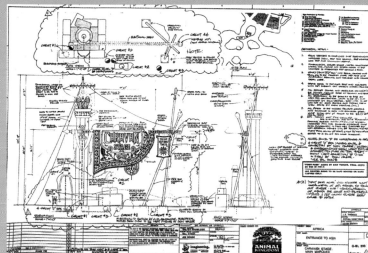

The Caravan Stage marquee contract document (above, left), design intent sketch (above), and finished product (left). The custom-painted "carpet" features bird motifs based on the avian show.

GORILLAS IN THEIR MIDST

The entrance to the Harambe Research Station—Gorilla Falls Exploration Trail—is really a cleverly disguised entrance to the aviary. "People will forget the overhead mesh—if they ever saw it through the vegetation," says architect Janikowski, when they enter the research station and see its computers, radios, and maps, and the mole rat habitat, themed as if the researchers have just cut away a dirt bank to expose the colony. The rats are fascinating—and guests either love them or hate them. "Either way," says Janikowski, "we've taken your mind off the fact that you've entered an enclosed space."

The oxbow islands of Gorilla Falls provide two habitats, one for bachelor gorillas and a separate one for the gorilla family. The river has steep concrete banks that lean in. To make a gorilla-proof wall, the sculptors creating the rockwork tried repeatedly to climb it. Any protruding handhold was circled with yellow crayon and later obliterated. The resulting walls act sheer, but look natural.

The lush gorilla habitats on either side of the swaying suspension bridge create "one of the best immersion exhibits anywhere," brags landscape architect Jim Brighton. The most daring-seeming sight gag in the valley is the final view of the gorillas, through a curtain of bamboo. Guests can overhear their vocalizations and smell their unmistakable odor. It seems as if the powerful primates can just snap a few spindly stalks and join the throng of guests. In reality, a live clump of plants on the guests' side grows in front of painted, sculpted steel bamboo securely anchored 2 feet deep.

Above: steel bamboo, now disguised by living plants, acts as an effective barrier between gorillas and guests. Below: an early concept drawing for the research station.

VERY SPECIAL EFFECTS

The special-effects wizards at Walt Disney Imagineering fearlessly work with lasers, cryogenics, and fire. They use projection effects, fiber optics and video, smoke and steam—all to ensure that special effects mimic the real thing as closely as possible.

An Imagineering machine shop manufactures components built to the specs of the mechanical designers and production engineers. While computers and CAD drawings are an essential part of the process these days, the special effects designers still roar around the construction site in search of a missing screwdriver or wrench. They are mechanics first and foremost. "I learned under original Imagineer Yale Gracey," says Gary Powell, who oversaw the installation of effects for Disney's Animal Kingdom Theme Park. "Gracey's maxim was 'The best effects are the simplest.'"

For this "medium-level special-effects park" Powell's team assembled the largest fog system in Disney history. For Countdown to Extinction, dozens of small, distant meteor strikes are given physical presence by a single effect—a machine that forces out a dollop of air with a chest-thumping whomp capable of dislodging a hard hat—that is, once the $3 worth of hanging silk foliage was removed from the front of the $35,000 airblaster. "It's all part of test and adjust," said Powell, as the crew removed the offending leaves.

The most complex assemblage in the attraction is called the "toaster effect." Show designer Paul Torrigino used the guts of a toaster to create the twin time-transfer tunnel walls on the ¼-inch-scale Countdown to Extinction model. The nickname for the scenes stuck as they grew to two full-size corridors, each

HIPPOS BELLY UP TO THE BARRE

Inspired by the research techniques of a pair of real-life scientists who scuba dive in Kenya to study hippos, the Gorilla Falls underwater habitat provides guests with a chance to observe the big beasts up close. Researchers, the story at the park goes, have dammed up the river that runs through the savannah in order to get a good look at the habits of the "river horse."

The surprise is the hippos' beautiful underwater ballet. Slow-moving and stately or skimming along with their toes barely touching the bottom of the river, hippos are graceful inhabitants of their watery world.

The savannah river and Gorilla Falls are only about 100 yards apart as the crow flies, with a hippo barn in between. The hippos alternate between the Gorilla Falls habitat and the savannah, with the result that guests, like researchers in the field, will potentially see different animals at every visit.

hung with 40 programmable strobes, shot through with lasers and throbbing with luminite. Fog and projectors enhance the experience, which makes guests think they've traveled back in time 65 million years. The corridors include cascading sparks created by "basically a giant cigarette lighter," explains Powell. "We just scaled it up twenty times. It was simple!"

MANAGING CHANGE

As construction wore on, the project and construction managers initiated the delicate Imagineering process known as "managing change." Changes cost money and time, two precious commodities. Construction manager Scott Williams explains what sets the Imagineers apart from other builders. "We're trying to create stories for our guests. The only way to pull it off is to make it obvious and seamless. When a story seems to fall apart, a show producer may ask for a change, even though construction is underway or completed. That's one of the tough parts of our business—evaluating change requests from our creative partners."

Williams identifies three categories of change. The easiest to accept are changes that *must* be made. For instance, the original ramp from the giraffes' barn to their savannah habitat was deemed too steep for the animals to negotiate and thus a potential source of injury. Yet the grade had to be maintained to hide the tall barn directly behind the savannah. Once Williams and project vice president Walter Wrobleski authorized the expenditure in the summer of 1997, the team built a meandering pathway through new rockwork canyon walls.

Another change that's relatively easy to approve is something that, once built, becomes a "showstopper." For instance, the savannah overlook building initially was constructed with heavy vertical wooden timbers that blocked the view. Cutting the uprights and theming the ends cost time and money but solved the problem easily.

Less cut-and-dried are the "nice to have's," things that aren't necessary but are considered nice touches. Williams points to an early decision to create less-finished rockwork for the savannah, where heavy vegetation would surround it. "To make the rock of finished quality would have been wasteful. Instead we used that money to create proper conditions in the animal quarters— adding rough or smooth textures, eliminating handholds. We thought assuring animal safety was a higher priority."

The center of communications for the whole property, the radio tower in the background was relocated to accommodate Imagineers' request for a clear view from the savannah. This change didn't cost the project anything: the tower was slated to be moved anyway.

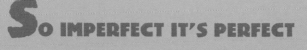

Sometimes things that seem authentic really are—like the roofs in Disney's Africa. Thatchers traveled from Zululand in South Africa to roof the buildings in the village of Harambe. The crew of 13 men sang while they worked. After tying together thick bundles of Berg grass harvested by their wives, sisters, and mothers back home, some crew members tossed the bundles up to the roof, where others hand-stitched them with twine, in traditional Zulu form—using 18-inch-long, half-inch-thick steel needles that are called "tulu."

At 70 pounds per square yard, the 4- to 6-inch-thick thatch on the savannah overlook alone weighed 2½ tons. "Grass is an unlimited resource," says master thatcher Val Deere, "natural, biodegradable, environmentally friendly." Deere, who has worked all around the world with palm, reed, and straw, prefers grass over other materials: "Grass lasts thirty or forty years, is fire resistant, and provides excellent insulation."

"Perhaps 60 percent of the buildings—everything from $15 million structures to mud-floored huts—are thatched in Kwazulu, Natal," says foreman Bev Walker, who lives in a thatched house in South Africa. "That's a pretty beam," meditates Walker, gazing at the underside of the train station roof. "The finish under here is important. This is where people spend time, and the thatch doesn't weather under here." The soft gold of the grass will mellow to silver in a few years' time on the outsides of Harambe's village buildings.

"You just calm down under here," explains Deere, walking from the hot broad daylight of a Florida summer at high noon to the hushed, soft dusk of the savannah overlook. "The thatching aesthetic calls for no corners—it's all soft, sinuous, undulating curves. It's so imperfect, it's perfect."

MASTERS OF PLASTER

The buildings that make up Harambe were designed by architects Eli Erlandson, Tom Sze, and Ahmad Jafari. The construction and materials are Swahili, and were inspired by a trip to Lamu, an island off the coast of Kenya, where many plaster-coated buildings are made from coral block. The Imagineers sent pallets of the bricks back to Florida, where they were cast in multiples and placed over steel frames. Then John Olson's character plasterers went to work.

Olson was an avid model railroad enthusiast while growing up in Anaheim, California, when he was invited to join a bunch of kids at the opening of a place called Disneyland® Park. By the time he joined Imagineering in 1974 he had a degree in marine biology and a business building architectural models. Many years of work on Disney parks, matching Epcot® pavilion exteriors to antecedents located in Morocco or Norway and creating treatments for made-up lands like Mickey's Toontown, has given

him a vast catalogue of treatments he shares with his team.

Rui De Matos works closely with Olson. The Portugal native learned the art of plastering when he re-created the walls of a ninth-century monastery and restored medieval frescoes. "You analyze everything you look at," he says. "Then you use it later." Native Floridian Gary Graham brings a wealth of experience and innovation to the team.

Olson, De Matos, and Graham create treatments for walls based on a building's age, use, and history—"the how, why, and what of a building." Three- by four-foot fiberglass replicas of cement, brick, and stone are light enough to be carried into the field when contractors duplicate brick-and-mortar, wood, or stucco finishes.

On-site, Olson and De Matos check for architectural integrity— Is the amount of cement sufficient for this joint? Does the building look like it's resting on the lowest stratum of rocks?—and make sure the cracks ("chicken feet," "lightning bolts," and other colorful monikers) make sense.

"I learned from Fred Joergger, one of the original Imagineers, that 'the first thing in building a rock is thinking like a rock.' I think like a building for the final phase," explains Olson.

His time machine is a high-pressure water hose. "It can give me seventy to eighty years of deterioration in about five minutes. It picks a weak spot and makes great little wiggles, like worm tracks." The Harambe train station has three layers of aging on four materials. The original building in the center is more weathered, with water damage where the eaves didn't protect the plaster. The wings, added later, are in better shape.

"We put a lot of effort at eye level," says Olson, "making things look accurate rather than contrived. Then we can do less at higher levels. The guests help us maintain the illusion, making up for a lack of definition at a distance with their imaginations."

MUSIC TO SOOTHE THE SAVAGE GUEST

"Music reaches a person on a whole different level than visual elements or text or the spoken word," says Imagineering media designer Russell Brower. It also reaches animals, and that was the jumping-off point for discussions about music in the park.

Media designer Don Lewis met with the team for the first time in July 1992. That initial exchange of ideas informed all subsequent sound design, making the design-

ers rethink how sound is used in a theme park. Live animals make their own sounds, which should not be drowned out. Adding random gorilla sounds was deemed a bad idea—the wrong sounds might make the animals aggressive or passive or just annoyed. The Imagineers vetoed anything phony—no blanket background music while guests are enjoying the animals, no lion roars when the critters are asleep.

The overall strategy that emerged was to blend music with environmental sound. On the safaris, sound is produced off-board (coming from the savannah rather than the vehicle) to give the illusion of activity in just a few areas—in the Ukungu Forest, at Hippo River, and at the savannah overlook.

Besides the resident animals, the park's source for sounds is Dr.

Bernie Kraus, a bioacoustician. Kraus and associate Doug Quin are artists and biologists, composers and scientists. Kraus has recorded a huge library of sound from all regions of the Earth, in all seasons. His randomizing technology, which Imagineering has adapted, enables the playback systems to go for months without a repeat. This is especially important for the animals. "We don't want to drive them crazy with repetitive sound," says Lewis.

Kraus also introduced the team to his "niche hypothesis"—the notion that each creature in the wild fills an acoustical niche, just as it fills a niche in the food web and the ecosystem overall. This theory helped sound designer Joe Herrington come up with an authentic roster of distinctive roars, squeaks, and growls for the behemoths of DinoLand, U.S.A.

LIFE ON THE TREE

"The Tree of Life brought those of us who do rockwork new horizons because it's so unique and important," says senior production designer and chief sculptor Zsolt Hormay. He put together an all-star team—"a left wing, a right wing, a center, and a goalie," as the Hungary native calls them—when he hired an international group of sculptors. Vinnie Byrne, from Ireland, and Fabrice Kennel, from France, joined Disney veterans Eric Kovach, Steve Humke, Joe Welborn, Gary Bondurant, and Jacob Eaddy.

Hormay also recruited a group of artists, who have their own studios and who work in a variety of media, to assist in creating the almost 400 animal images that make up the trunk of the Tree of Life. Roger White, an artist from Indianapolis, usually works in clay and bronze. Parker Boyiddle (his surname means "big light" in Kiowa) is well known for his 5-foot-tall, 2,000-pound sculptures of animals; he calls the tree "colossal!" Apache Craig Goseyun is a busy sculptor who works in the Southwest. Arapaho/Choctaw artist Arthur Rowlodge rounds out the "family." Hormay, who wears hishi beads and turquoise

jewelry in profusion, went after Native American artists "because of their feeling for animals—and because I've been intrigued with that culture since I was a five-year-old in Hungary."

The tree began as a half-inch model that was cut into 4- by 4-inch chunks scored in 1-inch cubes. A computer stylus was run down each line, and the drawings generated were burned onto a CD and sent to a rebar-bending machine that made the initial, crude "cages" in 8- by 8-foot steel sections. Welding the cages together provided the scaffold for the pencil rods—slim steel rods that formed the armature for the animals—a leg or face or foot. For 12 weeks the artists from Buena Vista Construction Company labored on the trunk, which was split into 12 sections—a double stack of six that would surround the oil-rig frame.

"If the armature looks good it's wrong," says Hormay. Proportion is built from the next layers—metal lath, like fine-gauge chicken wire, that provides the stratum for concrete, "the best medium in the world," coos Hormay. "With it, you can create a surface from glass-smooth to dirt and everything in between."

Between the metal-lath stage and the final application of concrete came the biggest logistical challenge—transporting the 12 individual sections from the welding yard to the Animal Kingdom site. In August 1996, a helicopter rose into the sky trailing each odd-shaped, almost translucent, 40- by 40-foot cage. Assembled on the site, the trunk went together without a hitch.

The Tree of Life was soon surrounded by scaffolding so the sculptors could get to work. Meanwhile, the branches were proving to be a problem: they

This page: a tree branch becomes an elephant's trunk as work progresses at the rebar yard. Opposite: assembling the cages (about 80 percent complete) around the lower trunk, before their transport to the site.

were too heavy. Eventually, the Imagineers came up with a three-part system: rockwork merging to carved foam, covered with a thin coat of plaster to match the trunk, then transitioning to resin. The different media were married with special joints so the branches could move in the wind.

After the engineers made them act lifelike, it was up to artists to make the branches look lifelike. Imagineer Gary Graham oversaw morning meetings as the sculptors met over a pile of wood for reference. They would discuss whether each branch should be "a banyan, an emerging oak, or a touch of cedar."

Today the 140-foot-high Tree of Life towers over the site. During construction, 10 flights of rickety stairs led up to the "dance floor," from which branches and leaves were mounted and sculpting began. Like Michelangelos of cement, the sculptors laughed off the physical danger. "You get used to it," declares Hormay. The artists worked on a scaffold—with planks about 6 feet wide—or roped themselves to the surrounding steel like mountain climbers. Painters followed sculptors, adding a rich palette of greens and browns to give the tree color. It sprang to life from the top down.

With nearly 400 animals in no particular scale, the challenge was to create images that seemed as if the Tree of Life had grown them spontaneously. A sea horse and an elephant are about the same size; so are the Florida icons, a manatee and an armadillo. A pile of sticks served as inspiration for the textures of the animals—the stripes on the tiger are banyan bark, and the octopus' skin is modeled on oak. Hormay's job was to keep the overall look consistent, and to decide who would sculpt what.

A vine morphs into an ant and a snake. There are geese and a herd of wildebeests, an iguana, a warthog, Kodiak bear, planula, dolphin, horse, and alligator—and lots of bugs in the *It's Tough to Be a Bug* queue line, which descends under the roots of the Tree of Life.

Chimpanzee researcher Jane Goodall visited the park-in-progress and wondered whether there was a chimp on the Tree of Life. Rick Barongi relayed the query to Hormay. Within a week, Hormay and Kennel created a perfect image of one of Goodall's most famous subjects, David Graybeard, at the entrance to the queue.

The team rooted out knotty problems—the horse's head was too big and had to be redone; a broken branch was reworked to reveal the interior of the upper canopy. As the work moved down the trunk, layers of scaffolding were removed, and the Tree of Life emerged. Florida's changing skies provided a constant light show, highlighting some animals and making others seem to move just on the periphery of vision.

In the final push to finish the sculpting, the team moved into the gnarled roots of the massive base of the Tree of Life and the "bug queue" interior.

Parker Boyiddle, who aloft had sculpted the mantis, bats, eagle's head, and grizzly bear, found another forte overseeing pencil rodding. Bright sparks of arc welders framing his powerful torso, he says, "I like the problem of it."

Inside the queue, flying Pterodactyls hide an overhead air-conditioning duct. Steve Humke had been on the job for more than a year, keeping track of all the mechanics, the waterfalls, and the live-animal containments, finding solutions to hiding audio and lights, ducts and sprinkler heads. The near-gothic theater's concrete convolutions were designed by him to hide a myriad of effects.

The cement has "endless textures and solutions," says Hormay. The Tree of Life, which is covered in some places with cement moss, also has cement bug tracks embedded in its cement wood roots. The artists' bag of tricks included tools borrowed from the plaster trade—pipe and marging trowels—buckets of pebbles, and homemade tools like "wires on a bungee." Plastic added to wet cement creates wrinkles. The medium, in buckets and on mortar boards all over the sculpting area, is fun to handle. Like very

pliable clay or runny playdough, it keeps a shape while an artist plays with it. It sets in 5 to 10 hours.

Covered with bits and smears of cement, artist Craig Goseyun, who sculpted the elk, alligator, rattler, horse, and bobcat higher up, was puzzling over a stag beetle. Next to him, Roger White, the acknowledged bug master, joined Goseyun and Hormay to discuss a 3-foot scorpion perched on a root. "Keep the banyan going here—create wrinkles from the joints of the tail. The wrinkles fall the way the root turns, see?"

"When there's no muse, you suffer through, or someone comes in and kicks your butt into gear," says White. "You hang in there working. We keep each other's spirits up. We're a family, a team."

Arthur Rowlodge agrees from overhead as he sculpts a gnarly root. "Another team member gets you energized if you're stuck. Everything is so new—there are no preconceived ideas. The different tones are all melded as one. We spend a lot of time composing and orchestrating, trying to avoid redundancy. We try to work with one brain."

Jacob Eaddy walks by and concurs, "You need a lot of patience." Hormay sums up the team ethic for the Tree of Life: "If you have an ego, you're history."

Top: Parker Boyiddle, Arthur Rowlodge, and Gary Bondurant sculpt the wolf; bottom: Craig Goseyun (left) and Arthur Rowlodge create concrete details on the trunk; inset: a rhino emerges as if it is growing out of the Tree of Life.

GOING BUGGY

It's Tough to Be a Bug is a 3-D effects extravaganza dealing with the most numerous—and perhaps most despised—denizens of the animal world. The fast-paced, hilarious show, which is housed within a spectacular carved hollow deep within the Tree of Life, attempts to redress that imbalance with a healthy dose of humor and plenty of witty repartee.

Writer Kevin Rafferty (who confesses to a bad case of arachnophobia) met first thing with Advisory Board member Ray Mendez, an insect naturalist. "My job was to impart the facts about ten quintillion bugs in only eight minutes," explains Rafferty. "Ray said that, most important, they are responsible for our food, as pollinators, and they handle our waste. If it weren't for bugs we'd all be dead in six months. That impressed me.

"It was almost a matter of getting our special effects to match the bugs' effects in nature. All the acts featured in the show are based on what actual bugs do. There really, truly are acid-spraying termites," shivers Rafferty.

It was tough to get to *It's Tough to Be a Bug*. An attraction inside the Tree of Life appeared in many drawing-board incarnations. Then Disney CEO Michael Eisner was inspired by a movie being developed by Disney's Feature Animation Division and Pixar, creators of *Toy Story*. He suggested Imagineering look into it. The complex theme park show went together quickly with the cooperation of all three entities. It's the first time Imagineering has created an attraction that debuted before its movie inspiration, in this case *A Bug's Life*, slated for release at Christmas of 1998.

It's Tough to Be a Bug features an ant named Flick, and Hopper, a grasshopper with an attitude, from the film. Imagineering created a put-upon Acorn Weevil, "the Termite-ator," a quill-throwing tarantula, and a cast of hundreds of butterflies and beetles, ladybugs and larvae.

Some cast members appear on film, several as elaborate *Audio-Animatronics*® characters, and a few exist solely as puffs of air in the backs and cushions of the theater seats. Flyswatter special effects are provided by about 50 high-speed fans hidden 30 feet overhead in the theater's rockwork folds. When the acid-spraying termite seems to squirt you in the face, it's actually harmless water coming from the seat in front of you.

Bug gags abound in the show. The lobby features posters advertising *My Fair Ladybug* and *The Mantis of La Mancha*. Guests don bug-eye 3-D glasses to watch the presentation, and are reminded to take their "little grubs" by the hand as they exit, laughing.

Characters from It's Tough to Be a Bug, *clockwise from below: Chili, the quill-hurling tarantula; the stink bug, Claire du Room; the Acorn Weevil; the Termite-ator; Rolly the dung beetle.*
Opposite, below: in a frame from the film, Chili indulges in a little target practice, firing spines at the Acorn Weevil. "No one makes a fool of Chili, man. Come back here and die like a bug!"

A DECISION OF CHARACTER

As work on the park progressed, projections of attendance were revised upward, and a new attraction was needed. A popular feature of Disney's other theme parks is the opportunity to meet the characters. The designers of Disney's Animal Kingdom Theme Park knew they couldn't include Mickey Mouse or Minnie Mouse in Africa or DinoLand, U.S.A.; they'd be out of context.

So they created a special place for them: Camp Minnie–Mickey, a woodsy, 5-acre attraction, its charming path wandering by a chuckling stream. Open-sided kiosks, complete with lights for a family photograph, are homes for a rotating cast of characters.

Minnie's overgrown gazebo sits next to Mickey's rustic overlook; the bamboo-shingle and thatched jungle kiosk shelters characters from *The Lion King* and *The Jungle Book.*

The forest kiosk, made from six trees that seem to have grown together, provides a place where characters such as Flit, the Seven Dwarfs, and Chip 'n' Dale can greet their fans both young and old.

A CONSERVATION CONVERSATION

"It's happening, honey! We duked it out!" says Zofia Kostyrko, one of the original Imagineers on the design team, as she reviews one of her domains, Conservation Station. Here is where the many threads of the park come together: animals and humans meeting face to face, to encounter the challenges ahead.

Conservation Station is the home of the only place guests can actually make contact with animals—the Affection Section. The Imagineers had two reasons for placing it here. On the practical side, access can be controlled so that the animals aren't overwhelmed by too much affection—and too many guests. On the conceptual side, it was important to have a place at Conservation Station where the youngest kids could be turned on to animals. The way to do that, the Imagineers have always believed, is through direct experience.

Many of the attractions within Conservation Station were inspired by Advisory Board mem-

bers, like Karen Allen, who said, "We in the conservation business haven't been able to talk about what we do, but Disney will enable people to experience it in three dimensions."

At Conservation Station, vets and animal care experts will be part of the show—working in their "fishbowls" to demonstrate what it takes to look after our fellow creatures. Guests can peek behind the scenes into a wildlife tracking lab, a completely equipped treatment room, and the hatchery for birds and small reptiles.

Invertebrate and reptile recuperation rooms are next to two cheerful nurseries that Kostyrko painted "as if I were decorating my daughters' rooms." The sliding windows in the food prep area let guests help with—even sample—the day's menu.

Guests get a feel for daily animal care by zooming the remote video cameras at Animal Cam to sneak peeks

at animals on the savannah and in their back-of-house quarters. They can also view a library of births, transportation, acclimatization, and routine care.

Advisory Board members like Michael Hutchins of the American Zoo and Aquarium Association are passionate advocates for conservation. He sees Disney's Animal Kingdom Theme Park, and Conservation Station in particular, as a place to hook guests up with ideas and resources once they've been touched by the message. "People can do so much—understand the issues, vote, lobby, organize, join organizations, volunteer, educate their neighbors, and evaluate their own lives—as well as recycle and control consumption and population growth."

To get guests connected both globally and to their local zoos and conservation organizations, Imagineers created EcoWeb. "We are simplifying access to conservation action information on the Worldwide Web," explains Kostyrko, whose team worked with the Advisory Board to create the prototype. "You can find out about your hometown zoo or keep in touch with your favorite monkey."

Director of conservation and science Beth Stevens and her staff oversee the education side of Conservation Station. Cast members are trained to answer guests' ques-

tions on animals, the attractions, and general topics such as recycling. The main hall, a friendly space with lots of light and live plants, contains a rockwork stage for presenting to guests a variety of small creatures—snakes and lizards, small mammals and bugs. A hidden video camera is controlled by the cast member talking about the animal so that close encounters can happen "even five rows back."

Stories from Disney Wildlife Conservation Fund activities provided ideas for attractions, such as Eco Heroes and Rafiki's Planet Watch, so Conservation Station will return the favor. Every penny tossed into the Wishing Watering Hole, which rewards donors with animal sounds played back on technology developed by U.S. Naval Intelligence, will be directed to the Disney Wildlife Conservation Fund.

Opposite: exquisitely detailed bronzes of baby elephants in the Affection Section house high-tech hand-washing stations.
Above: photo-realistic images of endangered species like the black rhino serve as photo opportunities in Conservation Station. On the reverse of the images are facts and fairy tales that illustrate humanity's long and intimate relationship with the animal world.

ADDING STORYTELLING MAGIC TO THE MIX

Imagineering's in-house media production unit, called Theme Park Productions, does much more than just produce the films and videos found throughout Disney theme parks. The team of writers and producers is deeply involved in story development. Head of Theme Park Productions Tom Fitzgerald explains a typical process: "At a point in developing Conservation Station attractions, Michael Eisner said he wanted 'more Disney' in it. He said everything had to be a jewel, and he liked the basic ideas, but it needed more heart to go with its head—the messages about conservation."

The Theme Park Productions team came up with a list of the great storytellers in the Disney animation pantheon who were associated with the environment. Grandmother Willow was a natural to lead guests on an audio journey in Song of the Rain Forest. Rafiki, who could give important, serious messages without being a turnoff, became the spokesprimate for Planet Watch, where the presentation may be playful but the message is profound.

The team even considered using Ariel for the show about the ocean environment, Mermaid Tales Theater. But because the show called for the 3-D host to be a new "minimatronic" figure it was impossible to give the full range of animation kids would expect to see in their beloved Little Mermaid. So the team developed a new character, Shelly. Her script, written by Paula Kessler and Steve Spiegel, began with taping seven- to-nine-year-old kids as they looked at pictures of the ocean. That gave the writers authentic language for the young mermaid, whose two-legged friends are elementary-age environmentalists.

The Eco Heroes attraction did not lend itself to a host from the animated—or animatronic—world. The team wanted to provide guests with an authentic experience of having interviewed some of the most dedicated people in conservation today. Chimpanzee advocate Jane Goodall, dean of conservation biologists George Schaller, Michael Werikhe, who walked around the world raising money for African rhinos, and Melissa Poe, who as a nine-year-old began a grass-roots conservation group, "don't do it for profit but because they need to do it," says Kostyrko. "We adore sports heroes and pop stars. Why not elevate and emulate these people too?" Incorporating sophisticated voice-recognition technology and a series of prerecorded segments, the Imagineers came up with a video-phone concept that allows each Eco Hero to have a unique

Left: working with Eco Heroes, says Imagineering creative executive Paula Kessler (kneeling in foreground), was a "dream come true. I was sitting at Jane Goodall's feet, writing words for her. Both Jane and George Schaller have a real air of calm about them. You can see how they could spend days or months just observing animals. They see things beyond what most of us see."

conversation with each guest.

Capturing the peripatetic Eco Heroes on film was a challenge aided, ultimately, by the park itself. Kenya native Michael Werikhe faced cameras on the re-created African savannah while George Schaller stood in front of a clump of bamboo in the Oasis, a stand-in for the Tibetan habitat of the giant panda.

These bits of magic, added to stories that perhaps began with a more somber tone, will help guests make a personal connection in Conservation Station.

"This is the real heart of the message at Animal Kingdom," says Kessler.

"I don't know how someone will visit here and come out without a greater understanding of the challenges we all face."

One of the most dramatic presentations in Conservation Station is static and wordless: just inside the entrance is a wall covered by a startling photo-real mural of 600 larger-than-life animals. On the mural, vivid natural colors fade into monochrome. "The animals are vanishing into oblivion—it's a visual cue of what we're trying to do here, to make you aware," says Kostyrko. The final image is of a silverback gorilla, almost faded away. "After he had been painted, I looked at him and he looked back at me, expecting. I had a gripping in my heart," she recounts.

It's the heart that keeps coming up when designers talk about Conservation Station. They believe that our human love for animals, inspired by the whole theme park experience, will be galvanized into action by these attractions. As Kostyrko says, "Conservation Station is a real effort to set a new standard for communicating and connecting about conservation issues."

ANIMALS ON BOARD

Giraffes Miles and Zari moved into their back-of-house home at Disney's Animal Kingdom™ Theme Park just as a torrential spring thunderstorm let loose. The humans in attendance contributed to the falling water as laughter and tears celebrated the arrival of the first animals at the park. "Miles and Zari looked up with their big eyes, batted their eyelashes, and seemed to ask, 'Will you take good care of us?'" reports Imagineer Walter Wrobleski. "It was just as emotional a moment as opening day."

The first animals to become part of the collection at Disney's Animal Kingdom™ Theme Park arrived in the summer of 1996 at a facility in northern Florida. The two young giraffes, Miles and Zari, were dubbed the park's "ambassadors." Soon enough animals to fill an ark were arriving for quarantine and checkups. A staff of keepers cared for birds and monkeys, duikers and bongos, klipspringers and nyalas.

Two waterbucks arrived pregnant. The first baby, a male, was named "Waterick" for director of animal programs Rick Barongi, whose given name is Roderick. Two zebras foaled, giving birth to a male and female, and the diminutive dik-diks mated soon after they arrived. A tiny female was born in the holding facility.

As the animal care team began to acquire animals, they developed a questionnaire that keepers filled out with the animals' natural history, characteristics, preferences, and habits. This information helped during transport, and in acclimatizing the animals to their new homes.

Disney's Animal Kingdom Theme Park designed a state-of-the-art hoofed-animal trailer. Zoological manager Martin Ramirez drove the air-conditioned, heated van, which is equipped with infrared cameras that scan the trailer's stalls. Four stalls made of movable partitions accommodate animals of all sizes. And all Animal Kingdom holding areas are built so that the trailer, large trucks, and crates can socket onto the building.

"The ideal move is from barn to trailer to barn," says Barongi. But those moves don't just happen. For example, the Imagineers, the animal care staff, and a film crew pitched in to literally build a road at Miles's St. Louis barn to accommodate the Animal Kingdom trailer.

> **❝We're all in it for the animals. If I can save them some grief or trauma, or make them enjoy life more, I'll do whatever it takes.❞**
>
> *LINDA OWEN,*
> *GORILLA KEEPER*

Moves away from Disney's Animal Kingdom—far down the road—will include thoroughly conditioning animals to what a move is like. It's not just getting into a crate or a trailer. An animal moves from a stall into a crate; then the crate is picked up by forklift and loaded onto a truck. The motion and noise can be frightening and disorienting.

There's always a risk to an animal during a move. Hoofed animals can lunge and jump and seriously injure themselves. Kangaroos, which can break their necks because the bones that hold their head and spine together are weak, tend to jump and hit their heads on the ceiling of crates. Tight, low crates keep the 'roos from hurting themselves in this way. "Lions are easy. They just glare at you," says Barongi. Hippos are also easy, but "elephants are always tricky because they are so smart and powerful."

Animals are crated if they arrive by plane. "You worry about ventilation—whether they'll be too hot," says Barongi. Disney's Animal Kingdom gorillas arrived from Chicago aboard chartered Federal Express planes. Hippos and giraffes traveled in modified horse trailers. Some animals were moved in crates that are loaded on air-conditioned trucks.

Crates themselves are a specialized business. Built of 2- by 6-foot planks bolted to an exterior steel frame, they can weigh more than the animals they house. A crate for a rhino might weigh 2,000 pounds. Adding the rhino's weight of 3,500 pounds makes for a huge special delivery. One entrepreneur has built a special moving van, reinforced with steel, that he hires out to haul elephants on the highway.

SPECIAL PEOPLE

Months before Disney's Animal Kingdom Theme Park opened, even before most of the animals were acquired, the hiring of more than 300 animal care specialists began. The early arrivals worked in temporary quarters in what would become the Operations building, while Imagineers finished the staff's permanent offices at Conservation Station.

Zoological manager Joe Norton explains his job as "the first-line manager in hands-on animal work." He works for a curator, and in turn has keepers working for him. He's responsible for several hundred critters, from alligators in DinoLand, U.S.A., to cockroaches in Conservation Station. The fish at Gorilla Falls will also be under his care.

Norton's job takes him all over the park, which he now knows firsthand. It wasn't always that way. He followed the early progress of the Animal Kingdom park in cyberspace, keeping up

Above: the crocodile habitat as envisioned by Imagineers; the tilting bridge was moved to a later point in the safari.
Opposite: a close-up of the massive crocodilians, all smiles, today.

with it on the Internet, through chat rooms and bulletin boards. "I let people know I wanted to work here," he says. He contacted 200 professionals already affiliated with the park, letting them know he was interested. In the summer of 1997, Norton joined the staff at Disney's Animal Kingdom Theme Park.

Like almost all the animal care staff, Norton is "cross-trained"—that is, he's worked with a variety of species. His early zoo background was with mammals; eventually he worked with reptiles, fish, and invertebrates. "In smaller facilities, it's a need," he explains. "And I personally liked variety, so I wanted to work in different areas." He is also unique in that his degree is in business management. He picked up his animal knowledge in 21 years of on-the-job training.

Norton has a staff of experienced keepers, well aware of the danger in caring for crocodilians, whose jaws have massive closing strength but not much opening power. "When you've got their mouths closed and your hands around the snout, the mouth stays closed," he says. "But they can go sideways with their heads and do you some damage. Our first priorities are animal welfare and keeper safety, and in this case experience keeps everyone safe."

A unique reptilian habitat is the crocodile pit on the African safari, where 30 male Nile crocodiles live year-round. A layperson's concern about 30 huge crocs wrestling for dominance is quickly put to rest: it's usually the females that create dominance battles. Bachelor males tend to struggle over basking sites or food, but that's it. Crocodiles aren't endangered, so an all-male group made sense: about 18 feet at maturity, these are the beefy animals you expect to menace your vehicle on safari.

Enjoying a leafy snack, an elephant forages in the onstage habitat. Cynthia Moss, the world's leading expert on elephants, observed the elephant family and pronounced them relaxed, calm, happy, and contented. "It was my best day ever," says curator John Lehnhardt.

A MAMMOTH JOB

Perhaps the park's most dangerous job is working with the elephants. John Lehnhardt, the curator of elephants, put into place a well-structured program based on his lifelong experience with these large animals at the National Zoo in Washington, D.C., the Calgary Zoo, and Chicago's Lincoln Park Zoo.

Elephants are a special case for many reasons. "When things go wrong with elephants, they go wrong in a huge way," says Lehnhardt. His keepers will stay assigned to elephants since they are specialists, although "consis-

tency is maintained by the program, not a single individual," he says. Elephants have the same life expectancy as humans, so each animal is likely to live through many keepers. Lehnhardt's role is to choose the elephants for the park, hire the keepers, and set up and manage the program.

Lehnhardt is excited by the elephant facility at Disney's Animal Kingdom Theme Park, which is unique in the United States for its spaciousness. The 6-acre onstage habitat, with its 100 species of plants, provides conditions that are "close to them eating and foraging in the wild. I can see them browsing on it for twelve hours a day."

In this natural setting, the curator hopes for success in reproducing. There has not been an African elephant birth in an American zoo since the early 1980s. Officially endangered since 1991, elephants can rarely be imported. "Now we've begun the push to get our U.S. zoo population reproductive and self-sustaining," he says.

There is also space at Disney's Animal Kingdom park to hold a bachelor herd of male elephants. Lehnhardt explains that at six to ten years old the males get testy. They need to leave the family and form their own herd. "Just as in the wild, we can provide that home here." The male and family habitats are separate, yet the animals have a trunk-to-trunk contact point at a concrete baobab the Imagineers dubbed the "Love Tree." "I don't know if they'll use it for that," says Lehnhardt enigmatically, "but I think they'll enjoy it for other things."

Before the elephants arrived, Lehnhardt spent hours inspecting their barn, offstage paddock, and onstage habitat. Screws, easily manipulated by delicately powerful trunks composed of 100,000 muscles, were replaced by welded bolts. Shade was enhanced.

In assembing a family of elephants—something rarely attempted in the zoo world—Lehnhardt wanted certain things. The highly social elephants would be brought to the park only in pairs or triplets. "We wanted them to have a buddy," he explains, "to reduce the level of change." The females had to be in their early teens, be reproductively viable, and be housed in a zoo in North America. He collected detailed histories on his candidates for Disney's Animal Kingdom. "We don't want an animal who is not capable of socializing," he says. "We want a group that can get along cohesively."

"We've only just started to understand what's important to elephants behaviorally and biologically," sighs Lehnhardt. "We need to provide for and utilize their need for sociability." In the wild, a group is composed of related females and their offspring. Each herd is a family, complete with siblings that babysit. These animals are totally comfortable in a herd, yet in zoos they're usually isolated, and males and females are housed together even though they don't live together in the wild. At the Animal Kingdom, their natural behaviors can be accommodated, but "we still don't know enough," says Lehnhardt.

The job of elephant keeper is one of the most dangerous in the world; at least one death occurs each year in the small (600-keeper) world of captive elephant management. Disney's Animal Kingdom Theme Park will provide a "protected contact" elephant program that places huge pylons, mesh, or large horizontal bars between keepers and animals. It keeps the humans safe during cleaning, hoof trimming, veterinary procedures, and feeding. But the program is not just about barriers; its foundation is consistency and relationships. The first pair of elephants to arrive from the Point Defiance Zoo, in Tacoma, Washington, brought their human social structure with them. Zoological manager Gary Miller had worked with the pair for more than 14 years, raising them from babies. Bruce Upchurch, who worked at Point Defiance for years, joined the elephant keeping staff temporarily to provide continuity. Mary Ellen Sheets from Seneca Park Zoo in Rochester, New York, also joined the elephant staff.

> **❝We've never traced a single elephant's life span in the wild, since they live as long as we do. We're only now scratching the surface of knowledge about them. We do know that elephants operate on a sensitivity humans have lost.❞**
>
> *JOHN LEHNHARDT,*
> *CURATOR OF ELEPHANTS*

To get the elephants in at night, keepers call them by name and bang a drum. The extremely social elephants seem to look forward to reuniting with their human caretakers in the back-of-house facilities each night, where snacks and baths are the bedtime routine.

66If a rhino could fall in love with a person, Tex would be in love with his keeper, Deanna DeBo.99

RICK BARONGI,
DIRECTOR OF
ANIMAL PROGRAMS

Two types of rhinos thrill guests on the savannah at Disney's Animal Kingdom. White rhinos (above) live with birds and other hoofed animals in a large onstage habitat. The more aggressive black rhinos (right) have a dedicated compound along the river.

KEEPERS OF THE FLAME

Good keepers are legendary. They exude calmness in body and mind; animals are quiet around them. Often sporting injuries—blackened fingernails, deep bruises, various abrasions—keepers have a sixth sense about animals that is irreplaceable. They tend to be highly visual, able to perceive subtle changes in their charges. Bird keepers notice that "something's just not right"—a change in posture or perch preference, a ruffling of feathers. Good keepers think like the animals they care for, no matter how humble. An invertebrate keeper can study a space and tell where a spider will want to hang out—and where it can get out.

Keeper Deanna DeBo became a Florida resident at the same time as Tex, the young rhino she has belly-scratched like a favorite puppy since he was two weeks old and in her care at the San Antonio Zoo.

When Tex was moved to his new holding area at Disney's Animal Kingdom, the rhino was reluctant to get off his trailer, but the sound of DeBo's voice had a calming effect. Having been a part of his life, and vice versa, for more than two years, DeBo speaks of Tex almost like a family member, telling stories about his babyhood and bragging about his developmental progress. "When he was first born, he ran laps in his enclosure for exercise. He used to chase a marabou stork for fun. Now he has a favorite log that he likes to toss around and bury in the rhino wallow."

Gino, the magnificent silverback gorilla, in his onstage habitat. He is head of the family troop from Lincoln Park Zoo in Chicago that also includes two females—26-year-old Benga and 14-year-old Hope—and two young males—Hasani, Benga's 3-year-old son, and Jabari, Hope's newborn.

The gorilla keepers at Disney's Animal Kingdom are also typical of the breed: passionate about their charges, respectful of the animals' power, and grateful to be playing a part in caring for these sensitive, intelligent primates.

Of three gorilla keepers—Linda Cory, Charlene Nixon, and Linda Owen—two once wanted to be veterinarians. Owen studied to be a police officer, and Cory worked as a cosmetologist, typist, and insurance computer specialist before getting a spot in the Los Angeles Zoo's Keeper Training Program. Each reports that when they got the opportunity to work with gorillas they felt as if they'd come home.

Every day is different for the gorillas, say the keepers; it's the humans who have a routine.

When they arrive at the back-of-house facilities (at 5 a.m. or dawn, whichever is earlier), the keepers first run a visual check of the night quarters, looking for anything that might have happened since about 9 o'clock the night before. If medical attention is required (because of a cold or an injury), the attending veterinarian is called. Then it's medicine, vitamins, and breakfast for these vegetarians: monkey biscuits and a mix of lettuce, bananas, apples, potatoes, corn, beans, tomatoes, celery, green peppers, and tubers. The food is generally spiced, cooked, or cut differently each day, as varying food in any way seems to capture the interest of the gorillas. "In everything, variety is important," says Nixon.

Left: splendid in the grass, Gino observes his observers much of the time. For 16 years, he lived mostly indoors. His first foray into his lush onstage habitat was accompanied by a whoop of approval.
Opposite: Gino in close-up.

Food is scattered in the gorillas' back-of-house areas and in their onstage habitat so they can forage for it as gorillas in the wild would. Treats, given during training sessions and "just because," include frozen foods, popcorn or rice treats, and spices to smell and taste.

The keepers then shift the animals from their bedrooms, clean up the rooms (gorillas make huge nests each night; the group at Disney's Animal Kingdom each get a bale of organic hay every evening), and check their feces and urine. Nixon climbed into one gorilla's nest (he was safely in the next room) and reported that it was "nice and padded." When they saw that the silverback patriarch, Gino, prefers to sleep on the cement floor, the keepers asked for a similar, natural-looking nap-place for his onstage habitat.

Training sessions come next. The gorillas learn to present hands, arms, ears, and other body parts to the keepers for exams or procedures (taking blood samples, trimming fingernails). Keepers can often get a gorilla to hold still for a veterinarian. The primates enjoy the stimulation of the training sessions and the associated treats. As the dominant male, Gino spent early training sessions going up to the rest of the group to make sure they were okay. Over the first few months, Hope, who arrived at Disney's Animal Kingdom Theme Park pregnant with Gino's offspring, became more social, changing her behavior from aloof to friendly and curious, and became eager to "help" by carrying implements from the back of her bedroom to her keeper.

"Enrichment"—keeping things interesting on a daily basis—is the top priority for the keepers of these curious primates. Backstage fun includes ice cubes, fire hoses for climbing, and tubs to play with, plus barrels, balls, ropes, and buckets with stuff like peanut butter smeared in them to examine. It might involve a burlap bag stuffed with hay that conceals a box that holds a treat. The keepers, who admit to being obsessed with enrichment, are constantly scanning their environments for items to adapt for the gorillas' enjoyment. They trade ideas with colleagues at conferences and workshops and consult primate hotlines. And the resources at Disney's Animal Kingdom, which is staffed with top animal care specialists from America's best zoos, are incredible.

Keepers are extremely knowledgeable about their charges, spending hours reading and discussing the latest ideas for improving the well-being of captive and wild animals. Nixon predicted that the Animal Kingdom gorillas would love the moats that surround their onstage exhibits after she discovered ground-breaking research showing that lowland gorillas frequent water, wading in to waist-level to dig out water plants for food.

All that knowledge is put to good use when the keepers go onstage, answering guests' questions at informal sessions at Gorilla Falls. The interaction "keeps you on your toes. You get good questions that send you off in a new direction," says Nixon.

66Sometimes you'll have a stressful day—then going home you'll realize the privilege of working with these animals. In the future, if we aren't careful, they might exist only in picture books, and you had the privilege of spending your life with them.**99**

LINDA CORY,
GORILLA KEEPER

141

142

TRAINING AND DEVELOPMENT

As the hoofed-animal herds were assembled in their backstage quarters, curator of behavioral husbandry Marty Sevenich worked with keepers to identify leaders of each species group. These "alpha animals," some wearing radio-tracking collars so they can be located on their huge savannah enclosures, will help lead their cohorts in at night.

Sevenich started her career with marine mammals, whose training provides some basic concepts used for all species. On a break from her employment at a zoo, she worked with bird trainer Steve Martin (who coincidentally developed the bird show for the Caravan Stage at Disney's Animal Kingdom Theme Park). "I was used to working with marine mammals in a pool," says Sevenich. "You have to be a very sensitive trainer to work with free-flight birds. When they become spooked they fly to Toledo!"

Dr. Jill Mellen is the park's research biologist. Her interest in behavior stems from frustration about what's known ("not too much!") about how animals live their lives from birth to reproduction to death. She has done all her studies on captive animals, partly out of an aversion to roughing it, but mostly out of passion. "Zoos are important places for animals, and they are important places to get people excited about them. Zoos will exist, so let's provide the best environment possible," she reasons.

Behaviorists like Mellen work with keepers, zoological managers, and curators, who ask questions about how to provide the best physical and social environments.

Like keepers, behaviorists observe from the animals' points of view. Things they do in the wild may be impossible in captivity, but the basic motivating factors remain the same. If the desired behavior is for the antelope to hang out by the ride tracks, Mellen and Sevenich first look at the environment and determine whether it is shady and comfortable.

Another aspect of training and behavior is enrichment—providing things for animals to do all day. Like many things at Disney's Animal Kingdom Theme Park, this program is special. The habitats themselves are enriching, with their mix of animals and vegetation and views of other species, but there are also tricks that may be called into play.

"Most animals in the wild spend the majority of their waking hours foraging for food," says Mellen. "So how do we sneak food onto the onstage area so that it is exciting to find but looks natural to the guests?" For the gorillas and mandrills keepers freeze food in a ball of ice. When the ice (which guests' don't see) melts, the pieces of food drop out.

Animals come to the area periodically to look for food, as they would when foraging in the wild. Natural-looking broken tree limbs with leaves to forage and browse are strategically placed on the savannah, where there are also shade, sun, water, other animals, and people in vehicles—all of which provide interest. Offstage, keepers may provide pierced plastic balls that dispense grain as the animals spin them.

The brother of support person Barb Burkhalter is a fireman for the Reedy Creek Fire Department located at the Walt Disney World® Resort; his company's old firehoses, from the "Dalmatian Station," are used in the back-of-house primate areas as swaying climbing structures. "Remember,"

> **"Let's take care of animals' well-being and breed them, but let's also try to preserve species-specific behaviors—by maintaining elements in their environment that allow them to make choices and that motivate them. Let's preserve their natural behaviors, not the shell of those behaviors."**
>
> JILL MELLEN,
> RESEARCH BIOLOGIST

Opposite, above: giraffes cross the ride path in front of the safari vehicle; below left: a greater kudu leaps across the re-created savannah past deadfall branches; below right: Mohr gazelles, a species extinct in the wild, get a vantage point from a grassy rise.

143

Long, lean and lithe, cheetahs are the swiftest animals on Earth, capable of short bursts of speed up to 70 mph. In the 1960s, their spotted coats made them a frequent target of poaching. Today, their numbers are declining in the wild as hordes of safari vehicles pursue and surround the shy felines, forcing them away from their hunting.

says Mellen, "an animal lives in a 3-D environment. We need to go vertical a lot." Natural-looking grapevine perches will be hung in the aviary, and mealworms will be hidden in a mud bank where guests can watch soft-billed birds dig them out and devour them.

To ensure that the animals are seen by the guests, yet are safe, it's vital to evaluate where they spend time and to keep them away from hazards.

The first step, before the animals arrived, was to walk the habitats with zoological managers, curators, and horticulturists. Attractive watering holes, shade, and hidden feeders were placed in viewable locations.

As they introduced the animals to the savannahs and smaller on-stage areas, keepers built temporary fencing of plastic sheeting and pipes; for the rhinos, concrete barriers left over from construction were used. Introduced to their outdoor homes a little at a time, the animals eventually followed the fenced paths to go to preselected (and especially picturesque) places to receive rewards. When the fences are taken down, it's anticipated that the animals will follow the established paths and corridors—most of the time.

Says Mellen, "The overall guideline is the animal's natural history in the wild. We look at the role of spices, scent, and feces from prey species as interesting signposts for animals that use their sense of smell to a much greater extent than humans. The zoo setting is a different context from the wild. Animals come from a complex environment, and we may not know all the factors."

The elephant curator John Lehnhardt agrees. "We don't know enough about how elephants operate—is it by smells or visual cues or both?—to experiment with just smearing stuff around or providing recordings of vocalizations to get them to do something." So enrichment is creative, but cautiously so. After all, the animal care team members are dealing with irreplaceable, beautiful animals. Says John Lehnhardt, "The goal is choosing enrichment appropriate to each species and carefully measuring the impact on the animals' lives."

In the fall of 1997 Disney's Animal Kingdom Theme Park experienced the first of the inevitable changes that come with keeping animals—birth and death. Veterinary services director Dr. Peregrine Wolff tells the stories:

"When Gloria, a black rhino, came to us in June we realized immediately something was wrong. She was thin and coughing. We called everybody in the country who kept black rhinos, as well as equine specialists from the University of Florida—horses are rhinos' closest domestic relatives.

"The Animal Kingdom vets, consultants, zoological curators, and keepers brainstormed ideas for treating her. For two months, we tried everything we could think of. All we knew was that she had bacterial pneumonia and was not responding to our treatments. We spent a lot of time with her, trying to see what more we could do. Gloria developed an immune reaction, and her blood vessels became inflamed and leaky. On the last day, I was with her when she collapsed. I knew it was the end. Everyone felt horrible that we couldn't pull her through.

"A necropsy found that a stick—21 inches long and a half-inch in diameter—had gotten stuck in her intestinal tract, and had perforated her colon, diaphragm, and lung. The fact that she had lived so long with such a horrible injury just amazes me. Looking back, there's nothing we could have done even if we had known what was wrong.

"Later that year, something wonderful happened. Hope, a lowland gorilla, had come to us pregnant. We thought she would deliver in October. We were concerned for her and her baby since Hope had abandoned one baby at ten days and the next at six weeks.

"As Hope's keepers and manager worked with her she became much more engaged. They got her to pick up an object and retrieve it, hoping that would train her to present the baby for us to examine. We also tried to reinforce good maternal behavior before she gave birth.

"Hope delivered her baby the first week of November. We didn't see it, but the birth seemed to go just fine. It was a male, and we named him Jabari.

"He has a fantastic hair-do—it's piled up high, with a lot of white in it. At a month old he could pull himself up. All Hope wants to do is hold the baby and eat. And Jabari is nursing like crazy.

"Now that the vets are coming around to visit, Hope goes to a far corner of her bedroom but then comes and stands near us. She hasn't let go of Jabari yet, so we hope she'll be a good mother this time around."

OH, BABY

Natural behavior is desirable because the more naturally an animal behaves, in general, the more likely it is to breed. The animal care staff is extremely optimistic about breeding—they are planning on it to help increase the size of the collection from opening day's 1,000 animals to an eventual 2,000-plus capacity.

General curator Bruce Read is upbeat about the pitter-patter of little hoofs and paws, but he's also realistic: "Not all females like all males, and here, unlike in the wild, there are limited pairing choices. But we have space and can allow animals to come together in a natural way. If we allow normal behavior, they will breed."

Sometimes it's the sheer size of a group that determines breeding success. Curator of birds Grenville Roles aggregated a large flock of rare African flamingoes in order to enhance breeding. Most zoos around the country have at most six or eight. He traded Chilean and Caribbean flamingoes from the Discovery Island collection for 57 Africans in order to found a captive, self-sustaining population, one of the largest colonies in the United States.

Every breeding at the park will be a planned breeding ("hopefully!" says conservation and science director Beth Stevens). Male and female animals are paired for mating with help from Species Survival Plans and Taxon Advisory Groups. It's important not to breed indiscriminately; just because the animals *can* have offspring doesn't mean they necessarily should. Bruce Read points out, "Every animal born at a zoo should be connected with the ones in the wild, so that the animals guests look at are connected directly to the wild, to nature."

Some animals whose numbers are huge in the wild will never be

bred at the Animal Kingdom; for example, common waterfowl will be represented by males only. The whole troop of Nile crocs in the park are male. The cockroaches on display, thankfully, are sterile.

Disney's Animal Kingdom Theme Park will work within Species Survival Plan recommendations to breed rare animals to increase the gene pool available. When an animal habitat is proposed, the staff searches for species that have Species Survival Plans established. For instance, Chinese alligators are in need of assistance, as well as being the right animal for DinoLand, U.S.A.'s Cretaceous Trail, which features survivors of the dinosaur

era. Zoological manager Joe Norton hopes to breed them.

Maternity stalls—somewhat secluded, with heated floors—are provided in the back-of-house areas, but births on the open savannah will not be unusual.

Most animals can give birth unaided. Vet director Peri Wolff wants to conduct a well-baby check at 24 hours after birth. "But if we can't, we can't. They may be healthier for it anyway. I'm a firm believer in sunshine."

The zoo community has well-documented research that shows baby animals are a huge draw. "It's a part of how we view nature, from its beginnings," says Bruce Read. Since they will bring in stable groups of animals that have successful track records in raising young, Disney's Animal Kingdom managers expect most births to be uneventful. The nurseries at Conservation Station are there only for support; the animal care staff will do everything they can to return babies from the nursery back to their groups at the earliest opportunity.

RETIRE IN FLORIDA!!

Like any animal facility, Disney's Animal Kingdom Theme Park may someday run out of room.

Breeding will increase the animal population and provide individuals to swap with other institutions. Offspring of loaner animals will return to their original zoos.

Animal Kingdom curators and keepers will also take advantage of the "back 40"—a series of large paddocks for mixed species, visible at the north end of the safari, that will be used to house breeding males and serve as a "retirement village" for older animals.

Inevitably, animals will get sick, be injured, and die. Still Barongi worries, "We don't

want to make a stupid mistake. We want to establish a perfect track record."

When animals die, a necropsy is performed by the vet staff. They look at the organs, microscopically examine the blood and other fluids, and can harvest eggs and sperm if indicated. They may even have to sacrifice an animal in a large group if it's infectious, to find out what's wrong before an illness spreads. "We deal with life," affirms veterinarian Wolff, "but its reverse is death, and that's part of the circle."

Opposite: animal keeper Cathy Yarbrough feeds a baby nyala. The parents of these southern African antelopes "tuck" their newborns— hide them in the grass—for about a week until they are old enough to follow the herd.
Left: an infant female dik-dik, who will grow up to be slightly larger than the male of her species. Her elongated nose holds scent glands for marking territory.

DISNEY'S ANIMAL KINGDOM AND THE SCIENCE OF ANIMAL MANAGEMENT

Disney's Animal Kingdom will set standards for animal care and exhibition. But how will other members of the captive animal community benefit from their expertise? "I expect my curators and zoo managers to publish, and I'll encourage my keepers to publish," says general curator Bruce Read. "I'm hiring keepers with masters degrees. I want to use the knowledge that we all have here, and I want to disseminate it."

It won't just be data about breeding; everything about an animal's behavior will be recorded by the keepers in their daily reports. The usual information that all zoos collect, like dietary and veterinary information, will be enhanced by observational and behavioral data. Keepers usually store such information in their heads or in private journals. It traditionally comes out only at night over beers after work. "The Animal Kingdom rule is, 'You're dead if it's in your journal and not in our record,'" says registrar Lynn McDuffie.

"We want visual things you can tell somebody," says Mellen, the behaviorist. "Like 'This cat is mad when his ears lay down like this or his tail is erect.' I can't use the old response, 'Well, I just know.'"

"The important breeding material is so anecdotal," explains zoo manager Joe Norton. "The information is there, but traditionally it's not written down. Our keepers will be part of our structure and commitment and will feed this data into the system."

Over time, the animal care team will develop photo references, refine their descriptions—when is a leg-kick a leg-kick and when is it a knee-jerk?—figure out how to quantify an elephant's stomping, and describe a bird's vocalization. All the information, entered into computers by keepers, will go into a massive database that will be available to all the animal care specialists, "but fast," says McDuffie. "Often keepers complain that they supply the information and never get anything back. We want to get the information back into the keepers' hands." Such input will help morning and evening shifts of keepers maintain consistent behavior. It will help with breeding. And ultimately it will help other institutions and the animals they care for.

Two hippos share quarters with birds at Gorilla Falls, where guests can observe their graceful movements underwater and at close range. Other animals in the herd spend their days in a huge two-river habitat on the African savannah, where there is room for up to 30 individuals. Vegetarians that can weigh three to four tons at maturity, hippos can stay submerged for as long as five minutes. Young hippos even suckle underwater.

GETTING DOWN TO BUSINESS

Everyone who visits a Disney theme park is called a "guest" and is treated as such by the men and women—the "cast members"—who work there. Careful planning in disciplines from costuming to maintenance begins long before opening; the commitment to unrivaled experiences for every guest continues daily behind and in front of the scenes.

Imagineers provide the vision for a theme park. They design and build it, sustaining creative energy through years of development. The day finally comes when the place is "dust free"—when the Operations division takes over. They are now the keepers of the vision, the cast members on the front lines who operate attractions, sell food and merchandise, maintain the attractions, and greet every guest with a smile.

Bob Lamb, by now vice president of Lake Buena Vista Communities, Inc., was associated with Walt Disney Imagineering throughout much of the design process. Traditional theme-park employees—ride operators, food and merchandise sellers, custodians—and the animal care staff report to him. As the park was being built, Lamb was hiring his top managers and putting them in touch with the designers to soak up the spirit of Disney's Animal Kingdom™ Theme Park.

The genial Lamb, whose face creases into a smile at the slightest provocation, fostered a sense of fun and camaraderie. Silly events like a fall "Homecoming Parade" and more serious task forces and retreats helped staff groups come into focus. The serious side of operating a theme park—safety issues, people-moving, last-minute adjustments—was never lost sight of in spite (or because) of the Operations folks' infinite capacity for play. "There's a lot of messing around in this park," Lamb laughed during a good-naturedly raucous meeting. "Whatever makes them happy!"

> **66**_On a basic level, we need to appeal to all ages. The Disney touch—an element of magic and surprise, a commitment to quality—has to shine through. You have to get the story across visually, without using language. Sometimes I'll wear earplugs while I watch a show, to see if I can follow it._**99**
>
> DOUGLAS MAY,
> SENIOR SHOW PRODUCER

LET US ENTERTAIN YOU

The live entertainment group at Disney's Animal Kingdom Theme Park took a new approach to creating theater shows, music, even the traditional parade. They want events to be involving and interactive. "It has to be fun—we want to get across the humor without losing the heart and soul of the park," general manager and senior show producer Douglas May says. The overall theme of the park is a human celebration of the animal world.

The entertainment group started with 40 or 50 ideas, winnowing them down to 20, to finally come up with an animal entertainment menu that includes stage shows, a celebratory "procession"—a scaled-back, interactive parade through Safari Village—and "atmosphere entertainment" in which a band of actors or a single performer performs for guests on the "streets."

Directors, writers, and musicians began fleshing out the shows about eight months before opening day; producers, production managers, designers, and costumers joined the team in the fall of 1997. Casting took place around December. After six weeks of rehearsal and another two weeks of running the shows, they were ready to debut to a very tough audience: the boss, Douglas May.

Safari Village was designed not to accommodate the traditional Disney theme park parade. May's group contacted Swiss artist Rolf Knie to design traveling assemblages, as if the artists of Safari Village get together twice a day for the sheer fun of celebrating the animal world. The resulting "animal festival" mixes with the guests. "It's very intimate," says May. "There are insects, sea horses, birds you can dance with."

The interactive, involving entertainment created for Disney's Animal Kingdom Theme Park is a trend in the entertainment world, acknowledges May, and it happens to be "perfect for this park. Movies and TV are passive. With live entertainment you can participate in the story that's being told. Guests want to walk away with an experience," whether it's one-on-one interactivity with the Changeling, who takes on the characters of tales told by the Story Teller, or the slapstick of the Environmental Acting Troupe of DinoLand, U.S.A.

"A lack of Disney characters for this venue has really opened us up," declares May. His cast of actors includes a group called Hai Jenga (Swahili for "living art"), whose members look like parts of Safari Village until they detach themselves from buildings to spit water or blow bubbles. "I've reached out to pop composers and used classical music. I know we've done a good job when the audience quickly responds. You can see their faces and hear their laughter, and you know."

Above: at Camp Minnie–Mickey, visitors encounter live animals in the friendly forested setting of Grandmother Willow's Grove.
Left: creatures of the "animal festival" celebrate the wonder of the natural world in a fun-loving, music-filled salute to the animal kingdom.

HOT COUTURE

Disney calls its employees "cast members" for a reason. When working "onstage"—in a park or resort venue—these people play a role. They get into character well before stepping through the "Cast Members Only" doors. It begins when they don what anywhere else might be called a uniform. Here it's called a costume.

Because anything visible to a guest is considered "onstage," it's important to match the mood of the costumes with their settings. The clothing "enhances the space it's part of, yet doesn't upstage the setting," explains costume design coordinator Patty Dunne, who managed the process of designing and creating 62,000 garments for some 3,500 cast members at the Disney's Animal Kingdom Theme Park, as well as hats, belts, jewelry, and props. She oversaw the park-wide budget costume by costume.

To approach the creative part of costuming, Dunne and her designers, Marilyn Sotto and Donna Bailey, walked through the story of the park with Imagineer Joe Rohde well over a year before opening day. "We want to reflect the passion behind the venue," Dunne explains. Research came next—books and magazines as well as the Internet. Sixty-one different designs were ultimately created for the Animal Kingdom park.

"Joe Rohde had definite ideas about clothing. He brought us sample clothes he had collected from Africa and India, and lent us books. He would draw over our drawings during the design stages," says Sotto. The challenge for the costumers is to make costumes that are "adaptable without sacrificing authenticity."

Operations input goes into design too; they ask for, and get, functional things like pockets and aprons. Nothing is created that would get in the way of a cast member's ability to barbecue a rib or load a vehicle.

The animal care staff had a stringent list of criteria for the keepers' costumes—nothing could be "grabbable"; there could be no headgear, nothing hanging off, no cargo pockets. They wanted something different from khaki, but everything had to be very durable. If a keeper's appearance changes, some animals, like gorillas, won't accept the keeper, so no one can add to or change their costume. And everyone wants comfort, especially in Florida's hot, humid climate. The costumers want to get everything right the first time—each design is meant to last five years.

Costumes must be tremendously durable. In the central Walt Disney World® Resort laundry, costumes are passed through steam on hangers rather than ironed. The elements—cast members work in all weathers—are a consideration, as is general wear and tear. Costumers have never met a body they couldn't fit. Each design must be flattering to all figure types, and maternity and handicapped styles must be available. An individual costume must last a year. Each design features the Disney name badge so it's visible ("over the heart," says Sotto).

Fabric is bought in huge lots. Disney's Animal Kingdom Theme Park has an extensive custom-printed fabric menu. Dunne says, "New technology is in our favor." The designers created color art-work to scale—all-over bug or dinosaur patterns, overscaled "engineered prints" in which art is placed carefully on the garment according to size. The manufacturers send back strike-offs that designers check for color accuracy, register, and sheerness. Then the fabric is printed en masse.

Creating unique printed fabric (backgrounds) is part of the job of costume designers.
Opposite, top left: the women's food and beverage costume for Harambe's Tusker House Restaurant *and* Tamu Tamu Refreshments *is based on an African dress called a boubou.*
Top right: Tree of Life cast members wear an exotic unisex costume that bespeaks another world.
Bottom right: the Swahili legend on the women's costumes for cast members at outdoor food and merchandise carts in Harambe translates into English as "Everything's Fine—Delighted to Meet You."
Bottom left: for cast members at Chester and Hester's Dinosaur Treasures, fluorescent jeans are appliqued with dinosaur footprints.

Dunne's team ordered 20,000 yards—20 percent of the cloth in the park—of a soft fabric manufactured from wood pulp and processed with recycled solvents, and thus touted for its environmental soundness. Fabrics, trims, and buttons are sought at trade shows. Custom belt buckles are struck in foundries, custom cloisonné pins created. The costumes were sewn in Los Angeles and St. Louis from August to January.

Shoes are suggested for each costume; cast members may buy their own shoes from a shoe mobile according to recommendations that take into account aesthetics, safety, and comfort. Each costume carries a bar code that is swiped at the wardrobe building when the cast member picks up the costume.

As a rule, costumes for cast members who run shops and sell merchandise are brighter than for those who help with the attractions. Custodial and landscape cast want to blend into the landscape, but the sellers want to be identified clearly.

Chester and Hester's dinosaur hats, originally created just for cast members, were so hilariously appealing that Merchandise created models to sell to guests.

The costumes for Disney's Animal Kingdom Theme Park are innovative in their design, materials, and construction. Some include jewelry and accessories that let cast members develop a custom look. The most conservative costumes are for the animal keepers, and for cast members assigned to Conservation Station and the Main Entrance, though some of these feature panels of whimsical animal prints. Donna Bailey based the jaunty beret for guest services on Kenya National Park Service uniforms. Wildlife Express conductors got vintage hats that Sotto discovered stockpiled in a Walt Disney World Resort warehouse.

Because Safari Village cast members will be in the sun a lot, their costumes are created in a fabric that wicks moisture away from the skin. Bright engineered prints on the loose-fitting food and beverage dashikis complement the surroundings.

Imagineer Joe Rohde asked that the Tree of Life costumes be exotic. "You're in a faraway place," says Sotto, "with a theatrical, larger-than-life backdrop." The first quick sketch—a relaxed, dropped-yoke shirt tucked into flowing pants that button at the ankle and are secured with bright fringed sashes—captured what the Imagineers wanted. A bug necklace completed the whimsy.

Rohde also wanted variety for Boneyard cast members, who play students at a dinosaur dig. They can assemble an individualized costume using three colors of pants and shorts and two shirts, plus two types of hats and bandannas. In another first for Disney's Animal Kingdom Theme Park, the wardrobe department supplies props—belts, brushes, and trowels for the Boneyard, rubber gloves and "safety shield" glasses for the Countdown to Extinction attraction. Costumes for Chester and Hester's Dinosaur Treasures reflect the general silliness of the shop—button-on slogans for shirts, fluorescent dino footprints on pants, and crazy dino hats with bulging eyes and long tails.

ANIMAL U

All cast members at Disney's Animal Kingdom Theme Park go through an intensive animal orientation period crafted by curators of education Amy Groff and Kathy Lehnhardt. The two-day session, unique at Walt Disney World, will help everyone from ticket booth operators to horticulturists answer basic questions about the animals found in the park. Part of the animal consciousness training is environmental awareness—cast members get a "green etiquette" book about conservation practices.

Cast members assigned to Gorilla Falls and Conservation Station, in the animal-viewing areas at DinoLand, U.S.A., and around the Tree of Life, will be trained even more intensively. Like zoo docents, they will be expected to provide in-depth information on animal characteristics and behavior. The training includes practicing interactive "conservation conversations" that cover topics about the environment and animals. Fact sheets, the park's own intranet, and other cast members provide the fodder—which first appears on index cards and later is filed in cast members' heads—for meaningful encounters with interested guests.

OPS ART

Disney's Animal Kingdom Theme Park was turned over to the Operations division at the end of January 1998. A shake-down period of running the park without guests was succeeded by a "soft opening"—an unadvertised opening of the turnstiles for cast members' families. The small—and forgiving—audience allowed the crew to practice everything from entertainment to giving guests directions to the restrooms. During this time, cast members worked out protocols and estimated demand, based partly on past experience. But Disney's Animal Kingdom Theme Park is an entirely new Operations ballgame.

Jim MacPhee's tenure as a general manager began in 1995 when he helped Imagineers refine plans for the park. MacPhee has responsibilities that include Africa, Asia, and Conservation Station—a staff of more than 600. General manager Debbie DeMars heads a team of 1,100 in Safari Village and Camp Minnie–Mickey. Erin Wallace, general manager of DinoLand, U.S.A., and the Main Entrance, will employ 713.

The diverse "proprietors" of each area—Bob Lamb calls them "my three-headed monster"—spent days identifying the talent they wanted. "Ideally we'll find people with expertise," says MacPhee, "whether in cleaning sidewalks or fixing boats." He hired self-starters, entrepreneurs. "I've told my people in Harambe that I see us as a 'chamber of commerce,' all helping each other, and with a bit of competitive spirit thrown in."

With Orlando's 3 percent unemployment and with high turnover in lower-level positions, the goal of hiring almost 4,000 cast members was daunting but not impossible. The managers planned to have about 85 percent of their cast members come from within the Disney ranks. When Walt Disney World cast members viewed a video that included scenes of the construction and a preview of attractions and costumes, they often greeted the film with an ovation.

"Everyone wants to work here," says MacPhee. "It's not just the lure of the animals. There is a cachet among Disney veterans about being on an opening team."

The big challenge goes beyond accommodating the demand to see the newest Disney theme park. Animals inevitably create a set of unknowns. "How long are people going to hang with the hippos?" asks MacPhee. "Our industrial engineers will be timing these things."

Another issue: daylight. It is expected that 100 percent of the park's guests will want to experience Kilimanjaro Safaris. The attraction is designed as a daytime experience, and "we worry about sunrise and sunset," says MacPhee. "Daylight Saving Time is a key factor in our opening hours." A tip board on display in Safari Village—a central listing of attractions and their waiting times—helps guests plan their time at the theme park. Extra shows and performers, scheduled at periods of peak demand, help keep guests entertained on even the busiest days.

> **Before we open, we walk through each part of the park, asking, 'What can go wrong here? How can we respond to keep the show running?' Being in maintenance kind of ruins the park for you.**
>
> JEFF VAHLE,
> GENERAL MANAGER OF
> SUPPORT SERVICES

KEEPING UP APPEARANCES

Maintaining Disney's Animal Kingdom Theme Park is the job of general manager of support services Jeff Vahle. His group of 300 includes engineers and custodians who face the challenges of running a theme park in addition to dealing with animals—elephants that shear off bolts, gorillas that bend steel bars.

For maintenance chores on the savannah—making sure the collapsing bridges are collapsing, the fog machines are fogging, and the fences and gates are intact—Vahle's team members are always accompanied by an animal keeper. Among the things they concentrate on are the relative danger posed by the animals (sable antelopes are among the more aggressive critters) and the fact that leaving behind a screw or a tool could result in gastric distress for an ostrich or eland.

Team members supervise life-support systems, including the water for animals off- and onstage. Yards of brightly colored pipes, punctuated by sand filters and ozonators, create circular mazes for the water systems, keeping the view clear and the environment healthy for fish and mammals. In particular, the hippo-viewing station at Gorilla Falls presents a huge technical challenge.

Structural integrity and safety are paramount. Then there's the subjective side. At Disney's Animal Kingdom Theme Park, Imagineering's vision of an aged, lived-in environment, a bit overwhelmed by nature, took some getting used to. Jeff's group, accustomed to rushing in with a paintbrush and touching up nicks and scratches overnight, has learned to take a more hands-off approach and to work with designers to determine when lived-in has become worn-out.

Planning for routine maintenance—for example, "rehabbing" the Tree of Life—began well before opening. The team started by evaluating the cost of special coatings to resist the sun and rain versus the cost of disrupting the flow of Safari Village for a month. Says Vahle, "If I can run conduit to a planned food or merchandise cart, I'll do it before the park opens, not after."

The attractions at Disney's Animal Kingdom Theme Park are both high capacity and high demand. That translates to a high maintenance load—shutting down an attraction during normal operating hours affects the whole park. The thrill attraction Countdown to Extinction is a known quantity in several ways, as its ride system is largely based on an attraction at Disneyland® Park. However, lurking in the blacklight are *Audio-Animatronics*® unknowns—new silicone skins, 3,000-pound hydraulic units, new show-control systems for the dinosaur stars. Two cranes will help the team survey the ride each night to spot potential problems before they become dino-size headaches.

Disney's Animal Kingdom Theme Park operates on an "ethernet," which is a park-wide fiber-optic network that controls every system—shows and attractions, background music, heating and air-conditioning, and computers for merchandise, tickets, and food. "It's cutting edge, the wave of the future—but I hope it's buried deep!" laughs Vahle.

Maintenance is like customer service, says Vahle. "We're serving the animal care staff and the operators, to make sure the guests have a great time. We want to be invisible. We want people to marvel at the park, not wonder when we're going to get something working."

Left: the interior courtyard of the **Tusker House Restaurant** *is reminiscent of an African bazaar.*
Lower left: *a concept sketch for tongs celebrating predator and prey, specially designed for the walls of* **Flame Tree Barbecue.**
Below: *a mosaic mural forms a dramatic backdrop for the* **Pizzafari** *kitchen.*

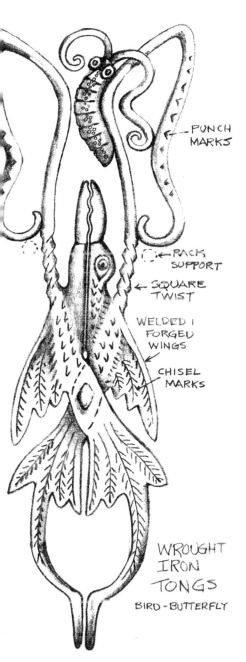

PUNCH MARKS

RACK SUPPORT

SQUARE TWIST

WELDED I FORGED WINGS

CHISEL MARKS

WROUGHT IRON TONGS

BIRD - BUTTERFLY

A GARDEN OF EATIN'

Food is a major part of keeping people happy at a theme park. Disney's Animal Kingdom chef Frank Abbinanti, who is a native of Palermo, Sicily, is an opening-crew veteran of the *Sci-Fi Dine-in Theater* and *Mama Melrose's Ristorante Italiano* at Disney-MGM Studios. He also has a strong commitment to quality and efficiency, designing menus that mix theme-park staples— burgers, hot dogs, chicken, and salads— in appealing ways. People are looking for a simple meal that tastes good and arrives quickly, Abbinanti says. There are vegetarian offerings in all quick-service facilities. And although "we don't try to reinvent the culinary world in a theme park," he is trying some new twists.

As a kid, "Francesco" would pull up a stool in his grandma's kitchen and help her make bread and pizza. The outdoor foods program at Disney's Animal Kingdom Theme Park allows guests to smell the aromas and see the action as cast members sell funnel cakes, caramel corn, burgers, and pretzels. Tossed-to-order salads are mini-shows. For *Flame Tree Barbecue*, Abbinanti and his lead chef Hal Taylor headed off to pit master school in Kansas City.

They learned a lot—"enough to develop our own barbecue sauce. We entered a contest and smoked meats for thirty-six hours in the middle of a field," recounts Abbinanti. "Nobody there knew we were from Disney. We took second place in the open competition for our orange trout and got an honorable mention in brisket." One of the fruits of the chefs' labors is a special Disney's Animal Kingdom line of barbecue products.

SELL SELL SELL

Food in a theme park needs to be recognizable, familiar to guests from three to ninety-three. In the world of theme park merchandise, however, differentiation is everything.

Ninety percent of the merchandise in Disney's Animal Kingdom Theme Park is themed to attractions and characters within the park. Everything on sale there will have a Disney's Animal Kingdom logo or identifier, from talking animal backpacks to a pith helmet surmounted by Mickey Mouse ears.

Brand manager Bettina Summermatter's team of product developers, artists and planners worked with Operations, Imagineers, Entertainment, Costuming, and Marketing to stock the park with tempting things to buy. Imagineers briefed the team on the park's overall philosophy before the product developers brainstormed. The Merchandise team decided that everything on sale in the park would reflect the human love of all animals—and the fact that Disney characters love animals too.

They started with 42 themes, visiting zoos, retail shops, and gift shows. In a tribute to the animals, they used spots and stripes for high-end apparel and home decorative items. Safari Village inspired a colorful line of women's apparel. Kids' items were tied in to the rain forest. The team came up with more than 3,700 pieces for kids and adults, including food and candy, media products, home decorative items, souvenirs, and soft lines (hats, clothes, and plush) manufactured all over the world.

Mickey Mouse and the gang have special safari outfits, and the Pooh crew is on safari as well. Disney's Animal Kingdom Theme Park scored a first in Disney merchandising: the large figures of Mickey Mouse, Minnie Mouse, and Goofy are standing. And Mickey is found in several unexpected places: leopard-like spots on a sophisticated line of clothing have a certain subtle, three-lobed pattern.

Summermatter also initiated a series of synergistic moves that let guests take a piece of the park home with them. Working with the Imagineers, she utilized art from Safari Village buildings to decorate products from tee-shirts to decorative home items, and recruited production designer Zsolt Hormay as a consultant for

Among the hundreds of concept sketches created for exclusive-to-the-park merchandise are these capturing the artistry of the Tree of Life (snow dome design, opposite page) and the whimsy of DinoLand, U.S.A. (bottom), as well as sketches that explore the possibilities for Disney's classic characters (left).

Tree of Life merchandise. Lifelike soft-latex dinos (available in small and large) are modeled on Imagineering interpretations of the creatures for Countdown to Extinction. The park's costumes inspired cloisonné pins and safari hats at DinoLand, U.S.A.

Concerned with the overall message of the park, Merchandise contributed to Disney's Wildlife Conservation Fund by creating the Add-a-Dollar Campaign and special shopping bags. Summermatter concedes that the most fun she and her team had was shopping for Chester and Hester's Dinosaur Treasures, with the license to develop and source the "wackiest and tackiest" dinosauria.

"Key drivers," tee-shirts that inspire guests to enter a shop for a souvenir, and "category killers," Disney's top sellers from all the theme parks, are the sturdy foundation of the Merchandise pyramid. The mix at Disney's Animal Kingdom Theme Park includes infant wear and gorgeously detailed snow globes, Balinese carved-wood objects, and African soapstone carvings. Summermatter and her team tapped into Disney's Animal Kingdom stories so early in their merchandise development process that every piece has a story, every piece tells a story, and every piece contributes to the story.

GREEN THOUGHTS

"There's always a wave of enthusiasm that flows through the whole company when we open a new theme park," says Walt Disney Attractions president Judson Green. "Imagineering has presented us with a fascinating theme park to entertain millions of people. Michael Eisner is incredibly proud from a creative standpoint. And there's a feeling that Walt and Roy Disney, the founders, are looking down and smiling.

"Disney's Animal Kingdom is entertainment, but it would feel empty if we didn't have the passion and the breadth of knowledge. This park may go beyond even Epcot® or the Disney Institute in terms of its educational value," predicts Green. "That's one of the many reasons we've attracted so many talented people from both within our company and from the outside. Besides delivering a theme park experience, we'll be impacting others' lives."

Green's personal involvement with conservation issues has led him to believe that Disney's Animal Kingdom Theme Park will make a tremendous contribution to public awareness. He's awed by predictions for Earth's population: 2 billion people in 1930, 5.7 billion today, 10–12 billion 20 to 40 years from now, with the period from 1930 to today causing the most ecological damage in history. "There's not a better time for conservation organizations to make a difference," says Green. "And we'll be raising awareness, offering creative ways for the guests to get involved and to connect directly with the conservation world."

A KINGDOM DEDICATED TO CONSERVATION

"In the end, we will conserve only what we love. We will love only what we understand. We will understand what we are taught."

BABA DIOUM,
SENEGALESE CONSERVATIONIST

The Disney Wildlife Conservation Fund helps animals and their habitats around the globe.
Clockwise from top left: elephants and Mount Kilimanjaro; young harpy eagle; green-winged macaws; cheetahs; an okapi and researcher; tree kangaroo; eastern needle-clawed galago; male iguana.

Conservation has been a part of the Walt Disney World® Resort since its inception in 1971. It stems from Walt Disney's own lifelong interest in and commitment to wildlife and wild places—the commitment that has inspired so many film, television, publishing, and theme park projects about animals.

The Walt Disney World Resort has set aside more than 14,000 acres to remain in its natural state as dedicated wildlife conservation areas and open space. Established in 1994, the Disney Wilderness Preserve, on 8,500 acres south of Walt Disney World, is home to the nation's second-largest concentration of bald eagles and 13 other protected species, including sandhill cranes, wood storks, and crested caracaras. The preserve, which consolidates vast tracts of land into contiguous acreage, is a living laboratory and a collaborative project among Disney, the Nature Conservancy, and government agencies—the first of its kind in the United States and a national model for other projects.

The Disney Company–wide *Environmentality* program, with Jiminy Cricket as its conscience-mascot, emphasizes conservation, waste minimization, education, awareness, and research. In addition to encouraging office-bound cast members to recycle, use E-mail instead of paper, and carpool to work, the ambitious program takes into account the workings of a vast resort kingdom.

Wildflowers have been planted along miles of roadways in Walt Disney World Resort to minimize mowing and create new natural habitats. The Bonnet Creek golf courses are landscaped with native species to reduce the need for irrigation, fertilizers, and pesticides. Wastewater is treated and used for irrigation or returned to Florida's aquifer. Compressed natural gas is used to power many resort vehicles. Electric vehicles are part of the fleet that includes mass transit for cast members and some guests. Ambitious energy audits and upgrades have earned Walt Disney Company the Green Lights Partner of the Year Award from the U.S. Environmental Protection Agency.

The recycling facility at Walt Disney World handles 37 tons of paper, plastic, glass, steel, aluminum, and cardboard every day. Even rafts and tubes from the water parks are recycled. Food scraps are used as livestock feed or are composted, along with sewage, landscape waste, paper, degradable construction debris, and ground-up wooden pallets—enough to make 50,000 pounds of compost daily. *Environmentality* buying encourages "green purchasing"—buying recycled and recyclable products and in bulk to reduce packaging and shipping.

Attractions also get into the act. The staff of The Living Seas at Epcot® studies and provides homes for endangered sea turtles and manatees. At The Land pavilion, plant cloning and fish farming are research subjects. The Land also participates with Walt Disney Imagineering's Research and Development group in an integrated pest management program. By using "good" bugs to eat "bad" bugs, they've been successful in reducing the use of traditional insecticides by more than 70 percent.

Above: Jiminy Cricket, conscience of the Disney Environmentality *program. Techniques developed by scientists at The Land pavilion at Epcot help control pests naturally. Ideally, "good" bugs eat "bad" bugs. Below, top: a lady bug attacks a cotton aphid; below, bottom: a lacewing larva with an indigo aphid in its jaws.*

Discovery Island has had success breeding protected species like white-crested hornbills and maguari storks, and the island acts as a protected rookery for native Florida birds.

A GREEN AND PLEASANT KINGDOM

The *Environmentality* continues on a daily basis at Disney's Animal Kingdom™ Theme Park, where the team's heightened awareness of threats to the world's habitats created policies in the construction trailers such as replacing disposable cups with washable glasses and porcelain mugs. And, of course, two-sided copying and recycling are the norm.

The *Environmentality* program at Disney's Animal Kingdom is officially overseen by conservation and science director Dr. Beth Stevens, and her staff members Kathy Lehnhardt, Amy Groff, and Kris Whipple. (They call themselves the Queen and Princesses of Green.) Groff, who is in charge of cast education, includes environmental and conservation issues in the unique two-day curriculum she has developed for all Animal Kingdom cast members. At the conclusion of this awareness training, each cast member signs an *Environmentality* Pledge that commits them to maintain an awareness of the wise use of resources.

Groff also handles internal matters, such as buying "green" coffee for the staff (it's grown in the shade and thus more friendly to migrating songbirds and other plants and animals). Lehnhardt's job, as curator of education for guest experiences, is to get the *Environmentality* and conservation messages out to visitors to the park. The cast members who work for her will be trained to strike up "conservation conversations" about topics of interest in

Gorilla Falls, DinoLand, U.S.A., and Conservation Station.

Composting is another big area of interest for the cast members managing animal care and the landscape. While currently they don't plan to sell "zoo doo," they will be composting the animals' bedding and manure. Using fish to keep the hippo pools clean saves cleaning and refilling them several times each week.

Ideas about recycling and conservation have become part of American life in the last generation. Most of us have become aware of how our habits—everything from littering to turning off lights—affect the environment. Disney has taken the ideas and ideals of conservation beyond its own backyard by establishing the Disney Wildlife Conservation Fund with support from the Walt Disney Company Foundation.

THE DISNEY WILDLIFE CONSERVATION FUND

The Fund's genesis was in the Animal Kingdom Advisory Board, a group of zoo and conservation professionals who impressed on Disney's top management the urgent need for the company to get involved with worldwide conservation efforts.

Defining conservation as protecting, preserving, and studying the environment, the Disney Wildlife Conservation Fund has granted millions of dollars to programs around the world. Each year an evaluation team from the animal management, zoology, conservation biology, and public affairs departments reviews applications and determines which programs will receive awards.

To qualify for funding, projects must satisfy specific criteria, which include contributing to the conservation of endangered or threatened species and their habitats through public education,

GOING LOCAL

Educating local people about the importance of wildlife is a key component of conservation thinking. Anyone who lives with or appreciates wildlife can keep it safe for the next generations, and outreach programs to share information about wildlife and ecosystems are essential. Through programs supported by the Disney Wildlife Conservation Fund, people who live in Southeast Asia have learned about bats, Brazilians have benefited from a rain forest interpretation center, and U.S. kids have learned about the black-footed ferret.

The Peregrine Fund supports research scientists in Madagascar with assistance from the Disney Wildlife Conservation Fund. The scientists often meet with bird-watching tourists on the remote island and ask them to donate money to the local school. The school principal teaches a lesson to students on where the money comes from. The message goes home to parents, who conclude it's a wise idea to keep the forests intact for ecotourism. In 24 months the researchers raised $500 (a fortune by local standards), which is being used to rebuild the school.

Madagascar red owls, once thought to be extinct, were found in the globe's last remaining coastal rain forest, the Masoala Peninsula in Madagascar, by Peregrine Fund researchers.

The Disney Wildlife Conservation Fund provided a base grant for Zoo Atlanta to establish a full-time conservation program based in Africa. The program's researchers found a live female Congo Bay Owl, a species previously known only from a specimen obtained 45 years ago. Researcher Thomas Butynski described his poignant feelings for the small chestnut,

buff, black, and white bird when it was released, and flew over a glade and vanished. "How many years would pass before one of the species would again be seen? Would we ever know what the male looks like or learn its call? Given the rapid loss of montane forest in Africa, was this the first and last time someone would hold a living Congo Bay Owl and see it fly?"

training, and research. All projects must result in quantifiable results within a year and must have a good probability of success.

The emphasis of the Disney Wildlife Conservation Fund is on field research and training. Money is given to support researchers or wildlife patrols, but not overhead. The goal is to support qualified scientists, educators, and organizations committed to preserving Earth's biodiversity. Of special interest are "biological hotspots"—areas of high biological diversity that are at the greatest risk.

The philosophy established by the Animal Kingdom Advisory Board is to make many small awards. "In country"—that is, in the field, which generally means in the developing world—a few dollars go a very long way. Numerous small grants spread the benefits among a variety of projects. Manager of con-

servation initiatives Kim Sams calls it the ground pepper rather than the peppercorn approach. She says "It's the best job in the world, knowing we can make a big difference even with a few thousand dollars."

PARTNERS IN CONSERVATION

Well over 150 projects, representing hundreds of animal species, have been beneficiaries of the Disney Wildlife Conservation Fund since 1995. Supporting nonprofit organizations that operate established programs has made it possible for the Disney fund to have an impact, quickly, around the globe.

Many projects are sponsored by organizations such as the American Zoo and Aquarium Association, which won grants for projects that are associated with its Species Survival Plans and that are designed to reintroduce reptiles to Caribbean countries, cranes to Japan, and lemurs to Madagascar.

Conservation International was given contributions toward their project to provide UNESCO biosphere reserves with Internet connections and basic training.

Defenders of Wildlife received funding to assist the Gros Ventre and Assinboine tribes in promoting tours of their bison ranges in Montana. The Jane Goodall Institute was given funding for a visitor center in Gombe that will help educate local people and international tourists about chimpanzees and their forest environment.

Veterinary and equipment supplies were purchased for mountain gorillas through the Morris Animal Foundation. The Peregrine Fund used a grant to study the harpy eagle, a "flagship" species for conservation of biodiversity in the neotropics in Venezuela and Panama.

Disney funds have been provided to the American Society for the Prevention of Cruelty to Animals; for lemurs at the Duke University Primate Center; for American Zoo and Aquarium Association wildlife and zoo staff training in Malaysia, Singapore, and Burma; to a Rio de Janeiro primate center project co-sponsored by the Philadelphia Zoo; and to an ongoing study of cotton-top tamarin distribution in Colombia.

The Wildlife Conservation Society used Disney money to conduct research on Bolivian macaws, Sumatran elephants, tigers, tapirs, and hornbills.

The Fund has also supported a project by the World Society for the Protection of Animals to vaccinate 20,000 domestic dogs around the Serengeti to halt the recent spread of canine distemper, which has killed about a thousand lions and other wildlife.

The Fund helped a Wildlife Conservation Society project that tracked forest elephants in the dense jungles of Cameroon and the Central African Republic. Field work such as this can be as frustrating as it is rewarding. A *National Geographic* writer traveled with researcher Mike Fay for several weeks without even a glimpse of elephants. He wrote: "We're in one of the last great wild places, and we barely understand how it works."

POINTS FOR BEING PRACTICAL

Disney money was used by the International Rhino Foundation to establish a Sumatran Rhino Sanctuary in Indonesia. The ambitious sanctuary is a managed breeding center and serves as a base of operations for rhino protection units in Way Kambas

66*Biological diversity is globally important. Its loss, an irreversible process, is the most critical issue of our times.***99**

DR. RUSSELL MITTERMEIER,
ADVISORY BOARD MEMBER

A Sumatran rhinoceros fords a river. Killed for their valuable horns, rhinos are unusual in that they are disappearing faster than their habitats. The critically endangered Sumatran rhino, like other rhino species, requires intensive protection and management.

PLACE OF SAFETY, PLACE OF STUDY

Field elephant studies are underway at Marakele National Park in South Africa. Disney has donated recently purchased land to the relatively new park, a rugged landscape of carved red cliffs and scrub forest. The closest national park to Johannesburg and Pretoria, easily accessible to a quarter of South Africa's population, Marakele is home to endemic and rare species of plants and animals. Plans for a youth education facility there will target city kids.

Marakele, which means "place of safety," was established in 1985 with scattered tracts of reclaimed marginal farmland amounting to more than 100,000 acres. The donation from Disney will help the park reach its ultimate goal: a coherent 250,000-acre parcel that incorporates the pieces of the current puzzle. As more land becomes available, ambitious plans are being developed for restoring the

original ecosystem by reintroducing native animal species that had disappeared from the area. Already on-site are 39 translocated elephants from Kruger Park, the future subjects of researchers at Disney's Animal Kingdom Theme Park. Once the elephants have had a chance to play their ecological role—tearing up shrubs and creating grasslands—the park managers will introduce other animals: first, grass-eating gazelles, and eventually various large predators, black and white rhinos, and zebras.

The nearby town of Thabazimbi, which supported the development of the first tented camp for tourism, sees potentially great economic benefits from Marakele. The park is a modern model of the conservation story: preservation, reestablishment of ecosystems, involvement of the local population, and subsequent sustainable economic growth.

National Park. The park prospectus contains a heavily fortified parking lot and camping platforms built on stilts 4 to 5 meters off the ground to protect tourists from "the frequent passage of wild and unruly elephants."

In the former Zaire, Delfi Messinger, working to protect elephants, decided to publish a blank school notebook featuring subtle conservation messages from Mark Twain, Karen Blitzen, John Donne, Cynthia Moss, Mungo Park, and even Alec Guinness. The project got off the ground slowly, and, Messinger reports, "there was a six-week delay due to lack of electricity at the printer." However, the notebooks, once printed and distributed, were a big success.

ACTING LOCALLY, ACTING TOGETHER

For many conservation projects, the involvement of local people and governments is essential for success, and the Disney Wildlife Conservation Fund supports this philosophical approach.

Recipients of this type of funding have included Conservation International, for training a

group of Belizean, Guatemalan, and Mexican biologists who monitor changes in Mayan tropical forests, and for promoting international partnerships that preserve wildlife corridors stretching across political boundaries in South America.

Under the auspices of the African Wildlife Foundation, the Amboseli Elephant Research Project in Kenya relies on local Masai tribespeople to help track elephants and document their behaviors and movements. In an okapi wildlife reserve in what is now the Democratic Republic of Congo, researchers found four new plant species, thanks to the collaboration of pygmy natives, a university-trained student who had grown up in the forest, and a western-trained scientist who was funded by Disney.

BEYOND MONEY, AWARENESS

Organizations that the Fund has been able to help are clearly making a difference for environments around the world. Yet there's much more the company can and does do. Jane Adams in Disney's Government Relations and External Affairs office actually gets to give out the checks. "It's wonderful to give money away. I wish I could call twice as many with the good news. But beyond the dollars, people are excited about tapping into Disney synergy. The extent of our reach is important to them."

Other Disney business units will help promote conservation: *Discover* science magazine regularly focuses on animals, insects, and issues related to ecosystems. *Disney Adventures* magazine runs conservation features with a kid-friendly focus. The Disney Channel brings a variety of wildlife programs to millions, including shows hosted by *National Geographic*'s Spin character and an engaging lizard named Henry. Short features have been produced for the Disney Channel about the work of the Wildlife Conservation Society and Conservation International, the African Wildlife Foundation, and the Peregrine Fund. A "pre-premiere" of the Broadway musical

MOST IMPORTANT: THE ANIMAL KINGDOM ITSELF

The Walt Disney Company realizes one of the greatest contributions it can make to global conservation is raising awareness. Walt Disney Attractions president Judson Green says Disney's partners in conservation are eager to join forces because "they recognize a company that can reach millions and millions of people."

Advisory Board member Michael Hutchins of the American Zoo and Aquarium Association feels certain that Disney can make conservation "a household word"; Terry Maple of Zoo Atlanta thinks Disney's Animal Kingdom Theme Park will effect a global change in the way people think about animals and their environments.

Animals are timeless, fascinating, moving. The Animal Kingdom park, by doing away with traditional barriers, dramatizing human-animal conflicts, and instilling a sense of fun, has the opportunity to convert guests into committed conservationists.

Judson Green thinks a new generation of Eco Heroes will result: "We'll have the opportunity to tell the stories about people who have the passion. I think we'll be motivating children by the hundreds every day."

Advisory Board member Karen Allen, a conservationist and mother, concurs. "Even the littlest kids can get the message. They may not be able to articulate it, but they will leave with a conservation conscience, knowing there is something big out there that can be part of their world. The Animal Kingdom park will change how they'll view the world for the rest of their lives."

The Lion King was a fund-raiser for the Wildlife Conservation Society.

Guests can make a direct contribution to the Disney Wildlife Conservation Fund when they visit Disney's Animal Kingdom through the Add-a-Dollar campaign, by buying special shopping bags and posters, and by "pressing a penny" at designated spots. All the money donated at the Wishing Watering Hole at Conservation Station will go to the Disney Wildlife Conservation Fund, as will money contributed by the human urge to chuck coins into any body of water (but hopefully not in animal enclosures!). This is no small change. Disney contributes nearly $100,000 each year to charity by scooping coins out of bodies of water at resort locations.

A LIVING LABORATORY

Research biologist Dr. Jill Mellen heads research efforts directed at understanding the behavior of the nonhuman population of Disney's Animal Kingdom Theme Park. Graduate students collaborating with keepers, zoological managers, and curators will publish papers in professional journals that will contribute to our collective knowledge about maintaining animals in optimal captive environments.

Studies of ungulates on the savannah will provide information about how they use their habitats, and will evaluate aggression between species (bongo vs. nyala, wildebeest vs. zebra).

Using sophisticated technology called the Geographic Imaging System, the animal care and horticulture staffs have teamed up to compile layers of data (shade patterns, temperature patterns, plant growth and decimation, and animal patterns) to monitor and maintain the savannah ecosystem of Disney's Animal Kingdom Theme Park. The detailed satellite surveys track plants and animals on each square foot of ground.

Elephants, hippos, and gorillas live in large social groups in the wild. They have been artificially, but—it is hoped—successfully, grouped at the park. Can a group of adults become a stable social entity? Through careful observation and trial and error, grad students, interns, and keepers will refine the emerging science of introducing members of the same species to one another.

Disney's Animal Kingdom graduate research fellow Kyle Burks works with the animal care staff to determine optimal grouping patterns and introduction schemes. Another graduate research fellow, Nancy Scott, leads a research staff in studies of chemo-communication and infrasonic communication among elephants that will provide insights into how animals communicate using sensing modalities that we humans can only imagine.

The Animal Kingdom park is funding a South African study of how closely related a group of wild hippos are. The results may help the animal care staff segregate its three hippo populations in the same way that they would naturally sort themselves out in the wild.

The wild-caught kori bustards are another unknown quantity. The birds will be equipped with radio telemetry equipment to monitor their behavior, activity, and well-being on the Animal Kingdom savannah. The bird staff will spend a year evaluating conservation-related projects to which they can contribute: massive reintroductions into the wild or more esoteric research.

Mellen, in conjunction with keepers and curators, is hoping to be able to record "first occurrences" for many animals at the park. This basic information—when animals go into heat or estrus, how long their gestation periods are, when young stand, eat and drink for the first time—is largely incomplete or altogether unknown. Disney's Animal Kingdom Theme Park could make a huge contribution to what is known about captive and wild animals by carefully documenting these events.

INDIVIDUAL OBSESSIONS

Research projects by individuals on Disney's Animal Kingdom team continue to make a contribution to conservation studies. General curator Bruce Read, in his "third year at a fourth try for a Ph.D.," studies the molecular genetics of the banteng, which are wild Southeast Asian ancestors of domestic cattle. Saving such wild species will help keep domestic herds healthy, says Read, whose undergraduate degree is in dairy science.

Conservation and science director Dr. Beth Stevens oversees research work by staff members both at the park and in the field. Conservation biologist Dr. Anne Savage, whose ongoing research in Colombia includes studying the reproductive biology of cotton-top tamarins, helps evaluate staff projects. Individual proposals will be subject to high-quality peer review. Savage looks for projects that guests can learn from, that are both "good science and good show," to feature in the Wildlife Tracking Center at Conservation Station.

Dr. Anne Savage (opposite page) monitors a cotton-top tamarin (above). While Savage uses sophisticated tracking devices to discern the habits of these South American primates, she advocates a low-tech approach to saving their rain-forest habitat. One of her field projects encourages Colombian families who live in the rain forest to use an efficient clay stove called a binde, which decreases the amount of wood they consume.

THE FUTURE: ANYTHING BUT CONSERVATIVE

Opposite, above: the Imagineers' original concept for Disney's Animal Kingdom™ Theme Park included an animal fantasy area with a toplary castle as a central icon. While not included in today's park, it could well be part of tomorrow's. Opposite, below: Asia is the first expansion of Disney's Animal Kingdom Theme Park. The Maharajah Jungle Trek will open in late 1998 with the white-water thrill attraction, and Tiger Rapids Run will come on board in spring 1999.

Even as guests were pouring into the entrance gates at Disney's Animal Kingdom™ Theme Park on opening day, plans for expansion were on the drawing board. Imagineers were still at work behind the scenes, in trailers behind DinoLand, U.S.A., on the site in Asia, and back home in California.

Industrial engineers had been studying the flow of guests during the months of "soft opening"—the unadvertised opening of the Animal Kingdom park. Usually family and friends of cast members, the guinea pig guests endured ride stoppages and halting spiels, minor breakdowns and major hassles, in order to say they were some of the first people to sample Disney's newest theme park. Ride operators and musicians, sous chefs and stockers, keepers and custodians all went through their daily routines with a purposefully smaller audience of guests until the tasks could be performed virtually without a hitch.

With the park running smoothly before opening day, Imagineers Joe Rohde and Jack Blitch consulted with vice president Bob Lamb. They knew that the Animal Kingdom park would have to be expanded; they had guessed this even before the park was announced in 1995. The Asian safari was already under construction in full view of the guests, whetting their appetites for a fast-paced white-water adventure set to open in 1999.

Tigers will be featured on the Asian safari.

Entertainment was planning to add musicians and comedians to "work the queues," a bonus for guests willing to endure the waits inevitable at a new theme park. Lamb's vision of a smoothly running theme park was every attraction filled and every queue line moving, with happy throngs of guests dining at restaurants and buying in shops. He needed more of everything to keep everyone, including himself, happy.

ANIMALS AHEAD

In the year before the park was to open, Rick Barongi's role had changed. Now he was in charge of animal programs development, which meant he held the vision for animals at Disney's Animal Kingdom Theme Park. He knew that some onstage habitats—for example, for elephants and gorillas—looked better the first day the animals were in them than six months later, after the inevitable "de-landscaping" had occurred.

Barongi looked ahead 5 to 10 years, when a herd of 30 hippos would "menace" the safari vehicle from both sides of the river; he planned to one day double the number of birds and mammals in the park, from 1,000 up to 2,000.

He knew the keepers and curators would be developing enrichment devices for the onstage areas to encourage behaviors, keep the animals moving, and keep them away from the delicate shade trees and foliage meant for "show" rather than forage. He anticipated having to move the animal cams to give Conservation Station guests a better view of what was going on behind the scenes and in the savannah.

Policy issues for the future were on Barongi's mind. He wanted the team to be able to welcome animals doomed in the wild if that was appropriate for the species and the park. But he worried that a possible negative reaction could stop such direct action. "We don't want to let the questions overshadow the commitment. We can't react to the individual finger-pointer out

there who has no credibility. Our vision will be realized if we don't hesitate in doing what's right, for us and for the animals."

IMAGINEERING THE FUTURE

With an available expansion area equal to the size of most theme parks, Imagineering creative designer Joe Rohde and his team faced an embarrassment of riches. The empty land south of Camp Minnie–Mickey and north of Asia could be used in many ways. The Imagineers sought the right mix of animal experiences and theme park attractions to keep guests intrigued and entertained.

A two-day "charette" was held upstairs at Disney's Boardwalk Resort less than a year from opening day. Its purpose: a five-year plan for the park. The Imagineers came up with a lot of fresh new concepts and confirmed the staying power of ideas dreamed up back in the early 1990s. An animal fantasy land was still a strong contender; it filled in the missing part of the Animal Kingdom concept "creatures that ever, or never, were." Safaris representing other parts of the globe, staged both inside and outdoors, were discussed. The fundamental philosophical split—rides vs. animals—would balance out within five years. But the question of what to develop first was, just like building the theme park initially, a question for corporate and Walt Disney World® Resort planners.

The best thing about planning for the expansion of Disney's Animal Kingdom Theme Park, says Walt Disney Attractions president Judson Green, is "the blessing of land." He expects that the creative direction will be influenced by both cast members and guests, as well as by "what's happening in the world. It connects back to the Disney Wildlife Conservation Fund. Something going on in the field is something we might dramatize at the Animal Kingdom. When the time comes, we'll open the creative spigot and let stuff flow."

Imagineering's vice chairman and principal creative executive Marty Sklar agrees. "We don't need a survey. Our guests will tell us very quickly what they want to see next. As Walt always said, 'We will meet the needs of our guests—and their expectations.'"

A ROOM WITH A GNU

South and west of the Animal Kingdom park, a parcel of land rimmed by trees was set aside to become a unique experience (tentative name: Disney's Animal Kingdom Lodge). With its very own herd of hoofed animals (antelopes, zebras, giraffes) and a gaggle of savannah-dwelling birds, the highly themed, upscale hotel would play host to guests who long to expand on their Animal Kingdom adventure by "staying the night with animals."

Every room in the hotel would look out over scrubland dotted with wild creatures; a giraffe might peer into your window while you dress for dinner. On a moonlit Florida evening as the animals gather around the watering hole, the illusion would be complete: a night on the African plains spent in grand style.

Designed by architect Peter Dominick, with advice from Animal Kingdom veterans Joe Rohde, Pat Janikowski, and Rick Barongi, Disney's Animal Kingdom Lodge would let guests bring a bit of "Animal Kingdom after hours" into their lives.

Among the animals slated for Asia are Malayan tapirs, whose young sport distinctive protective coloration.

ASIA, UP AND ALMOST RUNNING

Construction on the Asian safari was begun in summer 1997; it had been on the drawing board in one form or another since Disney's Animal Kingdom Theme Park was first designed. A 40-foot mountain of dirt—the highest point in the park except for the Tree of Life—was imported and carved into shape. Trees were planted on the crest and a concrete flume was poured long before guests entered the park.

Successive waves of Imagineers had visited festivals in Bhutan and gone river rafting in Nepal. Some had been elephant trekking in Thailand and had had pigment smeared and splashed all over them during India's Holi celebrations. The trips sometimes included Singapore, Bali, and Java, where designers photographed temples, rivers, jungles, and homes, soaked up ambiance, and researched issues.

The conflict between population explosion and traditional respect for animals and wild places was always borne in upon the Imagineers. Dramatizing it

without simplifying it was the challenge for show producer John Kavelin, as was including thrills for guests without traumatizing the animals.

Early on the team decided on a fast water ride and eliminated animals from the ride portion of the safari. Tigers were an integral and unchanging component of the nature walk, which included an evolving cast of wildlife that eventually included bats, tapirs, and exotic monitor lizards, as well as dozens of birds.

Guests will enter the village of Anandapur ("place of all delight" in Sanskrit) over a red brick bridge inspired by Nepalese temples. The village is the gateway to the Maharajah Jungle Trek and Tiger Rapids Run. The rafting company, so the story goes, is operated by local eco-entrepreneurs. Passing stately pillars and a temple surrounded by real bamboo scaffolding ("with gibbons who hopefully will be screaming at one another," says Kavelin), guests will enter a complex of Southeast Asian buildings that houses the queue line for the attraction.

Imagineers engaged in research will do anything in the line of duty, even subject themselves to the colorful celebration of Holi in India. Left: concept designer Zofia Kostyrko gets a dose of pure pigment in front of the Hawa Mahal in Jaipur, India. Opposite: Tom Sze took these photos of Varanese, India, as he traveled up and down the Ganges River in a wooden boat. The photos, connected to form a stunning panorama, inspired designs for Asia.

A HEARTY WELCOME TO TIGER RAPIDS RUN

The survey of Nepalese, Javanese, and Thai architecture begins with a tiger temple. A female voice will welcome guests to Anandapur and ask them to honor the traditional Asian respect for animals.

A covered courtyard, with a cobra fountain and animal sculptures in niches, leads to a spectacular painted pavilion, its ceiling supported by elaborate carved columns. Geese and tortoises, hares and banyan deer, lions and elephants, swans, jackals, lizards, monkeys, and crocodiles—all depicted in a delicate style reminiscent of Indian painted miniatures—cavort on the ceiling. The illustrations are adapted from classical Indian animal fables called the Jataka tales.

A bird shrine wraps around the painted pavilion. Birds there will include polylingual Greater Hill mynahs, speaking "polite expressions of joy and welcome," says confident birds curator Grenville Roles. The shrine leads to a shop dressed with "merchandise"—masks, kites, garments, pottery, objets d'art—all featuring animals. Live geckos will be "overrunning" one display case.

The Oarroom offers an orientation for the trip via a slide presentation. On the wall are oars

inscribed by intrepid adventurers who have gone before. The tradition is adapted from Katmandu's famous mountain climbers' bar, the Rumdoodle, where mountaineers sign Yeti footprints after they face the Himalayas.

Just before boarding, guests will get a glimpse of the rafting company office and hear the field radio warn adventurers away from a fire at an illegal logging site. But the warning comes too late, and the river journey begins. A dozen guests at a time will be boarded onto round, olive-colored rafts. A tranquil ride uphill, through a jasmine-scented curtain of mist and

past a tiger waterfall, is interrupted by a horrific dash through a landscape devastated by logging and burning out of control.

Imagineering special effects wizards warmed to their work, devising a spectacular flaming forest from pipe burners, fan burners, and an "accumulation unit" that throws explosive bursts of fire. An overturned truck on complex gimbals rocks at an odd angle; two huge logs swinging free overhead add to the terrifying scene as the raft spins wildly in the river. Then comes a stunning clincher: a heretofore hidden steep drop into a sheer-sided canyon ("it feels like the bottom has dropped out of the river," says Joe Rohde).

The drop was a subject of hot debate among designers and park operators. An innovation that had to be reengineered over the summer of 1997, it caused the ride opening to be delayed for a four-month period of "test and adjust." But as Imagineers and Walt Disney World employees rode the mockup in California, there was no contest. They think the thrill is worth the wait.

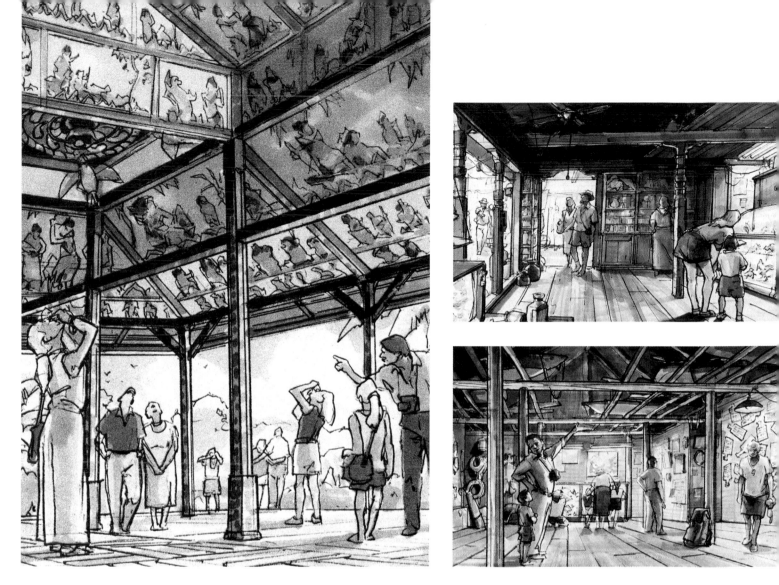

Scenes from the queue line complex
for Tiger Rapids Run.
Opposite, above: the entry court
puts animals on a pedestal; below:
the interior courtyard features animal sculptures in wall niches.
Above: the Jataka tales from India
were the inspiration for a magnificent painted ceiling; above, right:
the merchandise shop; middle,
right: the oarroom; bottom, right:
the authentic feeling office of the
fictional rafting company.

High water and high drama. Top: the raft begins its descent through burning forest; bottom: a sketch of the close encounter with a toppling truck and its load of logs.

MAHARAJAH JUNGLE TREK

A humble house marks the entrance to the Anandapur Royal Forest and its Maharajah Jungle Trek, supposedly created by locals to capitalize on some of the forest's natural wonders.

Reading a handout as they begin their trek, guests learn that the imposing Komodo monitor lizards (also called dragons) are relatively small representatives of the 12-foot specimens they will become. Tapirs live next to a facade of Indian folk architecture set into a rockwork canyon. And inside the canyon live the bats.

Bats are maligned and misunderstood in western culture, yet show producer Kavelin's design team and the animal care staff wanted to provide an incredible experience with these incredible creatures. They do allow those who don't care to expand their horizons an escape hatch, a straightaway that avoids the most amazing created habitat for flying mammals in the world.

The magnificent fruit bats—which have 18-inch, russet-furred bodies, intelligent canine faces, and 5- to 6-foot wings of delicate, veined skin—are essential for the pollination and propagation of plants in Asia. Flying in a figure-8 around their concrete canyon abode, the bats will home in on fruits and vegetables suspended from special animal-enrichment devices disguised as monument towers. The viewing room will be open to the habitat in places. The bats could fly out to join the humans, but they won't. While bats are being introduced to the habitat, the opening will be closed off with vinyl sheeting; that conditioning should deter the animals from deviating from a regular looping course.

The tiger exhibit devolved from a ruined hunting-lodge palace to an even more ruined hunting lodge at the behest of the Advisory Board. They asked the Imagineers not to present guests with walls, as that design called up visions of dreary, old-fashioned menageries. Instead they encouraged the Imagineers to tear down visible barriers to give the illusion that the tigers are freely roaming in a preserve shared with hoofed animals—blackbucks and Eldt's deer—that graze in the background. As at Gorilla Falls, guests will be on a bridge surrounded by wildlife. In Asia, the group of tigers will have access to both sides of their habitat via an underpass, which will be cooled in winter and warmed in summer so the cats will not linger there but will use it only for traveling back and forth.

The disguised "bird lock"—a decorative pavilion with a set of double doors that keeps birds safely inside the aviary—will afford another view of the tigers through its glass windows. Inside the aviary will be more than 50 kinds of birds—with ponds, waterfalls, mud walls for digging, and secure nesting sites.

The sheer diversity of Asian birdlife sparked curator Grenville Roles' imagination during the aviary's design and acquisition phase. "Asia is the quintessential fabulous bird place," he rhapsodizes, describing the jewel-like pittas, the dhyal thrushes and their glorious song, and wacky domestic forms of chickens like Phoenix fowl, which never molt their tail feathers. Asian aviary singers include silver-eared mesias and white-rumped shamas. Roles will even include birds that laugh: thrushes and Indian rollers. Green-necked lories and eclectus parrots will add color. He imagines his coletos, "bald birds with tasteful plumage, turning pink with passion or pale with fright." He expects the beautiful Bartlett's bleeding heart dove to prove a headache for the keepers. The bird has a pure-white chest with red feathers in the center. "Well-meaning guests are guaranteed to tell us we've got an injured bird," Roles predicts.

He expects most guests to be intrigued by the green pea fowl in the riverside habitat. Bigger than the familiar peacock, they sport glittering emerald green plumage and striking, naked blue and yellow patches on their heads. The peafowl will share quarters with banteng, the wild cattle of Southeast Asia.

Below: the Maharajah Jungle Trek features a tiger habitat complete with a pool and fountain for the water-loving felines.
Bottom: the aviary, home to more than 50 types of spectacular Asian birds, is styled as a palace being overtaken by jungle.

APPLAUSE

Top, left: the Operations leadership team for Disney's Animal Kingdom™ Theme Park. Top, right: the entire on-site Imagineering team photographed in early 1998.
Middle, left: DinoLand, U.S.A., Imagineers clown around on a Countdown to Extinction vehicle. Middle, center: the Imagineering design and production team, surrounding the Wildlife Express locomotive. Middle, right: Imagineers of DinoLand, U.S.A., standing in the Boneyard.
Lower left: the Imagineering team that worked on Safari Village, the Tree of Life, the Oasis, and the Park Entry. Lower right: the Africa team on the lion kopje.

Some books end with an appendix. This book ends with applause—a salute to some of the thousands of women and men who contributed their talents to the creation and day-to-day operation of Disney's Animal Kingdom™ Theme Park.

Noble in concept, epic in scope, the park was also a fun place to work. Crayfish parties and bubblegum-blowing contests helped take the pressure off. Disney cast members traded site sagas like baseball cards: On Valentine's Day at Gorilla Falls, a hard-hat marriage proposal in the midst of construction. A landscape manager dressing as a produce clerk for a meeting where he explained that the elephants were using his plantings as a salad bar. Young gorillas hugging each other as they entered their new homes. An African student seeing Harambe for the first time and saying she would no longer feel homesick.

There are the impressions of an author, given license to be a fly on the wall during design and construction: The puns flying thick and fast in a DinoLand, U.S.A., team meeting ("We're really sticking our necks out on that Saltasaurus"). The powerful, mysterious, spiritual intensity that the Tree of Life evoked in everyone who worked on it. The awe a layperson feels seeing wild animals up close, echoed by tears from a gorilla keeper as she tells me why she loves her job. A final sunset stroll through the African savannah before it became home to hundreds of animals.

Now merely a part of the general populace, I can say with the thousands of guests who experience this incredible place: Thanks for creating this three-dimensional love poem to the planet we share with the animals we adore. Bravo!

The DinoLand, U.S.A., team assigned dino monikers to its members. Show producer Ann Malmlund got the nickname "Vascilosaur"—described as "a highly developed ornamental nest builder"—for her trait of constantly redecorating her office.

IMAGINEERING TEAM MEMBERS

Charles Acevedo
Royce Acosta
John D. Adamczyk
Paul Adams
Mike Adcock
Frank Addeman
Claudia Addison
Francine L. Agapoff
Rajesh Agrawal
Joe Aguilar
Victoria Aguilera
Victor J. Aguirre
Christine Ahn
Charangsee Aiumopas
Christine Allen
Richard Allen
Carl Allison
Yusuf Almurdaah
Angelica F. Alviso
Leo Anderson
Todd Anderson
Vicki Anderson
Chris Andrade
Greg Andrade
L. Edward Andrews
Donna Anhalt
Frank Antonides
Greg Applegate
Pete Arcelona
Chris Archer
Frank Armitage
Karen Armitage
Nicole Armitage
Cheryl Arnold

Sally Arntzen
John Arreguin
Judy Ashbrook
Arden Ashley
Richard Atkinson
Raymond Avanessian
Amos Avery
Lyliam Ayon
Bruce Bader
Jerry Bailey
Brooke Baker
Doug Baker
Paul Baker
Bey Baldonado
Dick Bales
Jeffrey Ballew
Mike Barnett
Greg Barnham
John D. Barnhart
Wanda Barr
Bob Barragan
Beverley Barritt
Shane Bartley
Elmer Bashaw
Leo Bashbas
Keith Bearley
Keith Becker
Berj Behesnilian
Art Belanger
Carolyn Bellino
Miriam Ben Ora
Lee Benedict
Jennifer Bennett
Marissa Benson
Rick Berryman
Paul Bertram
Mike Bertrando

Rory Bestle
Barbara Bethel
Ronald Beumer
Brad Biben
David Bill
Diane Binford
Craig Birch
Michael Bishop
Alan Black
Jerry Blake
Bob Blanchard
Jack Blitch
Phil Bloom
Mark Bohlman
Bo Bolanos
Kirk Bonds
Sonja Bookman
Larry Borcherding
Brad Borgman
John Bradberry
Mike Brady
P. Gene Brady
Ashanti Branch
Robert Braunstein

*Patsy Tillisch,
associate producer*

Paul Bray
Casey Brennan
Cheryl Brickey
David Brickey
Jim Brighton
Russell Brower
Allen Brown
Kevin C. Brown
Larry Brown
Marie Brown
Michael Browne
Bob Bruggeman
Greg Bryant
Leeann Buckingham
Nancy Gee Bugman

Brian Burke
Don Burke
Donald Burke
Finton Burke
Bruce Butler
Donald Byrnes
Adella Cachu
Deogracias Calabio
Jose Camarena
Ruben Camarena
Tim Camaret
Tony Capelli
Steve Cardella
Seamus Carey
James Carlson
Cezar Carreon
Skip Carrillo
Marc Carsten
Jon Carver
Lynn Cary
Jim Casey
James A. Cashin
Celestino Cayman
Victor S. Chan
Bill Chaney
Deby C. Chang
Richard Chanowski
Wing Chao
Kathleen Charles
Maurice Chasse
John E. Chee
Jinn Chen
Joe Chesler
Jane Chiu
Abraham Chorbajian
Michael Chow
Kathleen Christie
Clifton Clark
Kim Clarke
Ursula Clemons
Ken Clinton
Oscar Cobos
Danielle Cohn
Judith Cohn
Lori Coltrin
Jeff Compass
Paul Comstock
Larry Cooper
Mila Corkins
Richard Cormier
Frank Cornalas
Robert Cortelyou
Jose Cortez
Sarah Costa

Noreen Coup
Antonio Cruz
Carole Curbelo
Aaron Currier
William Curry
Paul Curylo
Eric Daffern
Rick Daffern
Mick Dafters
Ray Dagala
David Dahlke
Elna Dane
Richard Davies
Mike Davis
Dick Dayer
Raymond De la Cruz
Gloria Del Toro
Judith Demarsh
Rui De Matos
Clarance Deruise
Duane Dietz
Mark Doege
Stephanie Donon
Jerry Dooley
Dale Doria
Janice Douma
Dave Dow
Edward Dowling
Duane Drake
John Dreher
Brett Dreves
Kristene Driver
Don Ducharme
Barney Dunn
Lyman G. Dunn
Consuelo Duran
Dave Durham
Robbie Durrance
Ernesto Dyquiangco
Jacob Eaddy
Ewart Earle
Eric Eberhart
Ron Edney
Curtis Edwards
Peter Egan
Paul Eisenbrown
Kim Erickson
Eli Erlandson
Ron Esposito
Doug Esselstrom
Kent Estes
Alex Estrada
Mark Andrew Evans
Eric Everettson

Will Eyerman
Mike Fagan
Alfredo Fajardo
Mina Farley
Dino Faucci
Russell Ferbrache
Bill Ferguson
Ian Ferguson
Sheena Ferguson

Writer Kevin Brown

Rich Fernandes
Nicholas Ferrante
Phil Ferraro
John Ferro
Pamela Fisher
Thomas E. Fitzgerald
Tom Fitzgerald
Jeff Flitman
Olegario R. Florendo
John Flores
Pedro Flores
Peter Flynn
Rick Fobare
Helen Fong
Brian Ford
Kelley Forde
Tom Fotie
Ira Frank
Arthur Franke
Don Fridlund
Ronni Fridman
Joel Fritsche
Jill Fukumoto
Michael Fuller
Melanie Fushi
Socorro Galam
Gloria Gannett
Blaise Gauba
Jim Gebhard
Jerry Geisen
Maureen Germain
Jennifer Gerstin

Jody Gerstner
Robin Gialantzis
Walter Gibson
Mark Gilbert
Eric Gill
Mitch Gill
Kerry Gilman
Chuck Girbovan
John Gizienski
Scott Goddard
Barry Golding
Art Goldstein
Fred Golshan
Kenneth Gomes
George Gomez
Jaime Gomez
Patty Gomez
Francisco Gonzalez
William Gonzalez
Don Goodman
Jenna Frere Goodman
Keith Goodrich
Joseph Goudeau
Cort Goudie
Gary Graham
Lizette Grau
Robert Grauer
Cicero Greathouse
Tom Griego
Wade Griffin

Dana Grobelmy
John Groper
William Guardado
Randolph Gueco
John Guerra
Alex Guerrero
Steve Gulati
Victor Gustin
Jaime Gutierrez
William Guy
Dale Hailey
David Hall
Tom Hall
Joanna Hamaguchi
Gordon Hamman
Brian Hammer
Melanie Hammond
Shannon Hanaway
Julius Hanke
Ed Hanna
Michael Hanson
Bo Hansson
Harold Happe
Pete Happe
Sharon Hare
Doug Harlow
Bob Harpur
Ron Hart
Brad Hartman
Gail Hash

Senior concept designer Zofia Kostyrko on Africa's Serengeti plain in 1990.

The Imagineers who created DinoLand, U.S.A., had creativity to spare. The team picnic table, carved over months with special slogans, found a home as a prop in the Boneyard. Seated around it are dedicated team members painting rocks for the **Restaurantosaurus** *rec* room. Left side of table: Bob Weiers, a photographer's assistant, Gary Powell, Lisa Stein; right side: John Sullivan and Nancy Izzo. Behind them, the van they painted with permanent flourescent lacquer during a team luau.

Dale Hashimoto
Paul F. Heath
Deon Hector
Thomas Heflin
Margaret Heiser
Paul Heitman
Ollie Hellert
Stefan Hellwig
Art Henderson
Bill Henderson
Teresa Henderson
Jim Hendrickson
Rick Hendrix
Shawn Henson
Peter Hernandez
Ben Herrington
Joe Herrington
John Hill
Mitch Hill
Clark Hinkel
Thomas Hogsett
Tracey Holloway
Christine Holmes
Matt Holmes
Paul Holmquist
Robert Holmquist
Elaine Holt
Conradine Holtz
Derek Holzer
Andrea Hom
Bahram Hooriani
Zsolt Hormay
Mike Horne
Alicia Hrabia

Julia Huang
Art Hughes
Darrin Hughes
Don Hughes
Steven B. Humke
Andrea Humphrey
Dale Hunter
Scott Hutcherson
Rachel Hutter
Richard Hutton
Paul Huynh
Sam Ingraldi
Tom Ireland
Jerrold Ivery
Patrick Ivie
Steve Izuhara
Nancy Izzo
Molly A. Jacks
J.J. Jackson
David H. Jacobs
Jay Jacobsen
Ahmad Jafari
Pat Janikowski
Bob Jeter
Brian Johni
April Johnson
George Johnson
Ronald Johnson
Debbie Jolley
Debra Jolley
Emily Jolley
Allen Jones
Darrell Jones
Kevin Jordan

Eric Jost
Mark D. Kallas
Glen Kaner
David Katzman
John Kavelin
Bret Kawashima
David W. Kay

Senior concept designer Zofia Kostyrko

James Kearns
Hovig Kelekian
Dana Kelley
Lisa Kelly
Fabrice Kennel
Rick Kess
Paula Kessler
Valerie Kevwitch
Jeffrey Kilbane
David Kilpatrick
Walt Kimes
Larry King
Jerre Kirk

Leslie Kirvin
Lori Klapperick
Gary Klebaum
Tom Kline
Vickie Knapp
Larry Knoll
Glenn Koch
Henry Kopecky
Zofia Kostyrko
Eric Kovach
Tristan Kuhlman
Vladimir Kulmaticki
Jess Kuncar
Ling Kou Kung
Jesse Kuntz
Robert Kuroda
Bobby Kurtz
Mike Kutcher
Paul La France
Doug Laher
Wes Lahey
Devin Lai
Robert Lai
Doug Lamb
Linda Lamons
Skip Lange
Michael Langston
Larry Lanier
Christian Lauren
Myron Lee
Peter Lee
Sabin Lee
Soo Lee
Roy Lemon

Mark A. Lescault	Ted Maesaki	Dave McCartney	Mark Miklovich
Marjorie Lew	Cynthia Mah	Mike McCullough	Steven Miles
David Lewis	Deborah Mah	Tori McCullough	Sherri Millard
Don Lewis	Trinh D. Mai	George McGinnis	Bill Miller
Jack Lewis	Leonid Makovoz	Bob McGowan	Chuck Miller
Jim Lewis	Ann Malmlund	Debbie McKinney	Eric Miller
Sue Lewis	Michael Margerum	Jodi McLaughlin	Jay Miller
Robert Liner	Jorge Marino	Rob McCafferty	Nanette Miller
Ulysses Lipa	Jennifer Marshall	Stephen McCalley	Scott A. Miller
Judy Liss	Chris Martens	Kevin McCarthy	Tammy Miller
Paul Liu	Richard Marthe	Terry McCartie	Paula Mills
Pat Loehr	Michael Martin	Iain McGillivray	Susan Milteer
Michele Long	Peter Martinez	Iain McKenna	Robert Minasi
Arthur R. Lota	Samuel Martinez	Jodi McLaughlin	David Minichiello
Deborah Low	Donna Masada	Marian McNair	Kim Minichiello
Margaret Lowe	Barbara Maslyk	Nelson Meacham	Diane Minton
Shihli Lu	Tom Masterson	Ana Medina	Moy Mitra
Alex Lubomirsky	Tod Mathias	Jim Medley	Elizabeth Mitsunaga
Mark Lucero	Mike Mathieal	Mike Mercado	Jennifer Mok
Amy Lucey	Chris Mazzella	Eric Merz	Lynda Montgomery
Charlie Lux	John Mazzella	Mark Mesko	Patsy Montgomery
Santos Luzod	Keith Mazzella	Maria Michel	Russ Moody
Earle MacVeigh	Larry McAfee	Alar Mikk	Fred Morita
			Mary Mosa
			Catherine Moulton
			Peter Mowery
			Gary Moyer
			Kurt Mueller
			Jim Mulder
			Joey Munoz
			Michael Murray
			Randy Myers
			Paul Y. Nagashima
			Hassan Naghipor
			Lonnie K. Nakasone
			Maureen E. Nehen
			Todd Neubrand
			Mohamed Newera
			Frank Newman
			Trung Ngo
			Dung Nguyen
			Hong Nguyen
			Liet Nguyen
			Phi Nguyen
			Linda Nikkhoo
			Nader Nohroodi
			Paul Norconk
			John Norman
			Chris Norris
			Armando Nunez
			Chuks Nwokedi
			Angel Olea
			John Olson

Chief designer Joe Rohde and show designer Jenna Goodman decorate rockwork on the African savannah with paintings based on Tanzanian petroglyphs both ancient and modern.

Katie Olson
David Orozco
Scott Owens
Jim Pacheco
Larry Paggeot
Tevy V. Pal
Alex Palaez
Troy Palermo
Odel Palmer
Doy Pamatmat
Portia Pamatmat
Patricia Parchmann
Maggie E. Parr
Richard Parskekian
Lisa Passamonte
Greg Paul
Bob Peppel
Roman Perez
Daryl Perkins
Robert Pero
Jerry Perryman
Debra Petersen
Ken Petersen
Selius Petit
Reza Pezeshki
Barbara Picking
Tom Picking
Decio Pinto

Jack Plettinck
Charles Pollard
Bob Pope
Nancy Porter
Whitey Pottruff
Gary Potts
Ardina Powell
Clifton Powell
Gary Powell
Tony Previtire
Matthew Priddy
John Pritchard
Kurt Pritz
Cappy Probert
Richard Prosser
Steve Pryor
Joseph Quick
Ramona Quinn
Cris Quinones
Gil Quintana
Behzad Rabizadeh
Margaret Rae
Kevin Rafferty
Roger Ramnath
Manny Ramos
Greg Randle
Jeff Rank
Ismael Ranzola

Landscape architect Paul Comstock caricatured on opening day.

Jack Raupach
Pamela Rawlins
Marianne Ray
Dominic Rayner
George Recalde
Ken Redford
Greg Reed
Paul Reedy
Jason Rees
Linda Regalado
Shawn M. Reifeis
Judy Resh
Freddy Reyes
Joseph Reyes
Philamer Reyes
Ricardo Reyes
Gabrielle Reynolds
Richard Rich
Wendy Richards
Tony Rienerson
Cyd Rincon
Daniel Riordan
Juan Rios
Peter Rios
Kathleen Risley
Cathy Ritenour
Rey Rivera
Stewart Robertson
Bill Robinson
Wayne Robinson
Alfonso Rocher
Melvin Rodney
Michelle Rodriguez
Ruben Rodriques
Joe Rohde
Ed Romeo

Waldo Romo
Mary Rood
Leland Rorex
Mike Ross
Steve Ross
Rick Rothschild
Steve Rotim
Brian Rousch
Arthur Rowlodge
Chris Runco
Peter Ruppel
Craig Russell
Debra Ruzinsky
Mike Sacco
Margaret Saginian
George Salamanca
Risto Salo
Hector Sanchez
Robert Sanchez
Uriel Sanchez
Chris Sandberg
Paul Sangha
Ernie Santacruz
Jorge Santamaria
Dan Sauerbrey
Ron Schaefer
Philip Schenkel
Barbara Scherer
Ken Scherer
Jack Schilder
Pam Schirmer
Ron Scholtz
Derek Schubert
Eric Schuh
Joan Schult
Mary Schutte
Jacqueline Scoggin
Rick Scott
Wray Scott
Alec Scribner
Steve Shaffer
Shawn Shahfar
Akram Shamsabadi
John Shaw
William Sheerin
Bita Sheibani
Larry Sheldon
Kevin Sherbrooke
John Shields
Matthew Shigihara
Taki Shimojima
Bob Shinn
Steven Shinkle
Eric Shipley

Gorilla My Dreams: landscape designer Dana Grobelmy accepted Harold Worthington's proposal at Gorilla Falls on Valentine's Day 1997. He got her there at sunset with an emergency phone call and surprised her with a picnic supper—and a diamond ring.

John Shipley
Lee Shipman
Kevin Shultz
Mark Shumate
Richard Simonton
Michael Sincavage
Daniel Singer
Surapol Singsanong
Marty Sklar
Les Skoloda
Tim Skundrich
Ralph Slay
Cecil Smith
Roy Smith
Nonilon R. So, Jr.
Stephen J. Sock
Nick Soricelli
Cesar Sotelo
Jose Sotelo
Kim Spaeth
Carole Sparkman
Richard Spencer
Robert Spencer
Jean St. Marc
Bud Stacy
Ginger Stanley
Cliff Starling
Lisa Stein
Judy Steme
Eileen Stephens
Robert Stephens
Tom Stephens
Russell Stokes
Tim Stone
Mary Ellen Streets
Richard Streitz
Robert Struble
Curt Strumlauf
John Sullivan
Maurine Sullivan
Michelle Sullivan
Rick Sutton
Eric Swapp
Tom Sze
Matthew Tager
Tony Tamalunas
Ken Tang
Dexter Tanksley
Ali Tarazkar
Steven Tatham
David A. Taylor
David J. Taylor
Rick Taylor
Michael Terwilliger

Brian Thomas
Jim Thomas
Laura-Susan Thomas
Wayne Thompson
Kyle Thurber
Patsy Tillisch
Tim Timsuren
Gary Tokumoto
Sebouh Tomacan
Phil Tong
Paul Torrigino
Chieu Trankiem
Michael Traxler
Benjamin Tripp
Patrick Truex
Mike Tseng
Celia Tubera
Bill Tyson
Rick Urick
Laurie Valadez
Anita Valjin
Jules Vallier
Rosemarie Van der Linde
David Van Wyk
Yifat Vapnik
Esau Varela
Jesus Varela
Joan Varelas
Jyssette Vargas
Phillip Vaziri
William Vedder
Pedro Velasco
Edmond Verloove
Marie Viglienzoni
Mario Villamayor
Erick Villanueva
Jose Villanueva
Jose Villegas
Ruben Viramontes
Teresa Viramontes
Alberto Vispi
Leanne Vogelgesang
Artem Voskanian
Kim Vradenburg
Jeff Wade
Brian Wagner
Jamie Wagner
David Wagoner
Richard Wall
Gary Wallace
Judith Wallace
Cal Walsten
Kristen Walton
Marianna Walton

The loquacious Joe Rohde, earrings flying, pitches an attraction concept to the team in this caricature by Ben Tripp.

Ji Liang Wann
Grace Warfield
Al Wargo
Jerry Wargo
Ray Warner
Bill Watkins
Dave Watson
Donald Weaver, Jr.
Bob Weiers
Harry Weiss
Joe Welborn
Mike Welch
Troy Weldon
Sally Wellingham
Barbara Welsh
Don Welsh
Ed Welsh

Matt Whipple
David White
Roger White
Joe Whitehead
Amy Whitman
Jeff Wildman
Bill Willcox
J. R. Williams
A. Scott Williams
Franklin Williams
Gary Williams
Heather Williams
Mindy Wilson Fisher
Steve Wilson
Henry Wines
Gayle Wise
Gene Wiskerson

Midway through construction, some Imagineers started sporting tiny, fluorescent compasses around their necks. The origin of the practice is shrouded in mystery, as are the reasons for each induction. Pausing outside their construction trailer are some members of the "cult of the compass." Back row, left to right: Doug Esselstrom, Jerry Blake, Tom Kline, Jenna Goodman, Miriam Ben Ora, and Paul Eisenbrown. Front row, left to right: Chuck Girbovan, Bo Bolanos. Not shown: Les Skoloda, Janice Douma.

Ken Wong
Howard Woo
Scott Wren
Alex Wright
Keith Wright
Phil Wright
Walter Wrobleski
Eileen Xie
Casey Yadon
Steven Yagade
Kenji Yamamoto
Laura Yates
Yvette Yessayantz
Eui Keun Yoon
Rhonda York
Celina Yu
Tom Zaczyk
Frank Zanaboni
Deborah Zanella
Johnny Zhou
Scott Zuber
Kietin Zyhal

OPERATIONS TEAM MEMBERS

Frank Abbinanti
Carolyn Argo
Rick Barongi
Cindy Barron

Michael Beatty
Dan Beetem
Bettie Belair
Roger Benyei
Andrew Betts
John Biava
Scott Blohm
Brian Bolstein
John Bradley
Darlene Brady
Donald Brannon
Troy Brown
Val Bunting
Barbara Burkhalter
Kyle Burks
Richard Carlson
Rick Carmean
Steve Castillo
Lidia Castro
Angela Cecil
Ray Christianna
Joe Christman
Jacqui Cintron
Angela Collins
Cathy Collins
Chris Cook
Carolyn Cooke
Linda Cory
Tanya Croft

Scott Daniels
Sonia Davidson
Deanna DeBo
Alyssa DeMaria
Debbie DeMars
Michael Dill
Deborah Donovan
Sue DuBois
Ramon Ducos
Eric Eberhart
Debra Edmondson
Susan Feltman
Debbie Frare
Barbara Gauger
Todd Glanz
Amy Groff
Alan Hall
Todd Harmon
Leah Havill
Paul Hawkes
Jeffrey Hawkins
Mary Ellen Heindle
Roberta Hejna
Dennis Higbie
Rick Hill
Barbara Howard
Michael Hudson
Liz Hurckes
Cheryl Jordan

Sharon Joseph
Joe Kalla
Walt Kimes
Ty Kirkpatrick
Gary Klebaum
Eric Lalin
Bob Lamb
Trevor Larsen
John Lehnhardt
Kathryn Lehnhardt
Ira Leonard
Avis Lewis
Dean Lofgren
Leah Logan
Mary Rose Luft
Jim MacPhee
Sharon Madill
Kathy Maley
Lisa Marshall
Jill Martin
Jim Martin
Cheryl McBride
Lonnie McCaskill
Lynn McDuffie
Scott McKnight
John McNaughton
Roy Mecklenburg
Farshid Mehradadfar
Fran Miglore
Bruce Miller
Gary Miller
Michele Miller
Jim Naelitz
Jamie Najera
Mark Natter
Patty Nichols
Charlene Nixon
Gary Noble
John Norman
Joe Norton
Jackie Ogden
Linda Owen
Connie Phillip
Chelle Plasse
Mark Potter
Nancy Pratt
Martin Ramirez
Bruce Read
Scot Reynolds
Jeff Ridout
Joe Rindler
Glenn Roberson
Doryan Rodriguez
Grenville Roles

Alan Root
Anne Savage
Vicki Sawyer
Marianne Schum
Terry Scruggs
Rhonda Semones
Marty Sevenich
John Seybert
Brian Sheets
Joseph Sherwood
Shelia Sherwood
Neil Simmons
Christy Sky
Debbie Snow
Juliet Solanzo
Tracy Sorensen
Mark Stetter
Beth Stevens
Bettina Summermatter

Jean Therien
David Thomas
Lorie Thuesen
Scott Tidmus
Bruce Upchurch
Jeff Vahle
Jeff Van Buren
Susan Van Metre
Erin Wallace
Martha Weber
Doris Welder
Keith Wittaker
Peregrine Wolff
John Wright
Tao Xie
Cathy Yarbrough
Kathryn Yochis
Lyn Yucuis
Bob Ziomek

Zsolt Hormay, senior show production designer and chief sculptor for the Tree of Life, trained in Hungary as a fine artist, and is also an accomplished Native American and Hungarian folk flutist.

Ben Tripp (whose face is hidden in the river bank, lower right) assigned his fellow team members animal identities in this portrait of the "surviving species" of Disney's Animal Kingdom™ Theme Park. Writer Kevin Brown surveys the scene from a tree above show producer Ann Malmlund (left, the triceratops) and landscape architect Paul Comstock (the lion). Senior concept designer Zofia Kostyrko perches on the safari vehicle while show designer Paul Torrigino and architect Pat Janikowski gaze past assistant Jennifer Gerstin, the caracal cat. Landscape planner John Shields is the elephant, associate producer Patsy Tillisch the giraffe, show producer Kelley Forde the honey badger, and team leader Joe Rohde the orangutan in the foreground.

THE ANIMAL KINGDOM INDEX

Understanding the logistics of building Disney's largest theme park can be approached through numbers. Here are mind-boggling figures supplied by Imagineers who managed, designed, and planned the park:

Cubic feet of dirt moved on site: 4,400,000
Miles of pipe at Disney's Animal Kingdom Theme Park: 60
Average number of feet of pipe laid per month: 100,000
Feet of pipe laid per day: 5,000
Feet of pipe laid per day, per crew: 350
Peak pipe day, expressed in number of crews: 17
Peak pipe day, in number of feet of pipe laid: 25,000
Largest diameter pipe, in inches: 84
Location of deepest utilities, in feet underground: 28
Gallons of water moved in park per day, overall: 15,000,000
Gallons of water that contacts animals, per day: 2,600,000
Animal Kingdom water-table depth, in centimeters: 30–45
Average rainfall at Disney's Animal Kingdom site, in inches/year: 50
Groundwater fluctuation at Disney's Animal Kingdom site, in feet/year: 3–4
Gallons of water in Discovery River system: 27,000,000
Square feet of rockwork: 1,000,000
Miles of retaining wall: 6.5
Miles of electrical conduit: 600
Thickness of concrete walls in gorilla building, in inches: 12–15
Air exchanges per day in gorilla building: 16
Beam height of giraffe building, in feet: 20
Panes of glass laminated together at gorilla-viewing windows: 5
Depth of gorilla-viewing windows, in inches: 3
Weight of doors in elephant barn, in pounds: 20,000
Weight of doors in hippo and rhino houses, in pounds: 10,000
Linear feet of track in Countdown to Extinction: 2,400
Vehicles in Countdown to Extinction: 16
Animated dinosaurs in Countdown to Extinction: 19
Animated pteradons in Countdown to Extinction: 3
Miles of cable and wire in Countdown to Extinction: 70
Plastic dinosaurs in Chester and Hester's Dinosaur Treasures: 1,407 (and counting)
Miles of cable and wire in entire park: 2,500
Imagineering-produced construction drawings for Disney's Animal Kingdom park: 7,000
Plants installed, site-wide (approximate): 4,000,000 plus
Species of grasses installed site-wide: 300
Vetiver grass shoots planted: 46,202
Shrubs along route of African safari: 771,687
Estimated number of 1- to 2-inch thorns per inch on the umbrella thorn acacia: 4-8
Average growth of new shoots of bamboo, in inches/year: 480–600
Age of cycad species, in years: 67,000,000
Average days of frost in central Florida, over 10 years: 3–5
Average days of frost in central Florida in 1996: 9
Weight of largest living transplanted tree, in pounds: 168,000
Average thickness of baobab tree at maturity (200+ years), in inches: 200
Average thickness of baobab on opening day (3–4 years old), in inches: 6–7
Pounds of pressure per female elephant: 10,000
Reach of an average browsing giraffe, in inches: 216
Depth of elephant ditches, in inches: 120
Average height of an elephant, in inches at the shoulder: 144
Leaves on the Tree of Life: 102,583
Weight of the Tree of Life, in pounds (approximate): 4,000,000
Weight of the Tree of Life, with cast members and guests, in pounds (approximate): 4,085,000